The Happiness Equation

The Human Nature of Happy People

The secrets of what makes us happy are revealed through our evolution,
and a unique Ipsos consumer survey of everyday Canadians.
Discover the drivers of natural happiness, and the importance of caring.

John A. Hallward

Library and Archives Canada Cataloguing in Publication

Hallward, John A., 1961-
    The happiness equation: the human nature of happy people /
    John A. Hallward.

Includes bibliographical references and index.
ISBN 978-1-897336-49-6

    1. Happiness. I. Title.

BF575.H27H35 2011   158   C2011-903623-1

Published in Canada by Price-Patterson Ltd.
Canadian Publishers
Montreal, Canada

Graphic & artwork design: Ipsos Marketing Services Unit
                    and John A. Hallward
Book layout & design: Ted Sancton/Studio Melrose

CONTENTS

Walking Along the Evolutionary Path
Evolution Has Wired Us To Pursue Happiness
Our Big Brain Causes a Psychological Problem
Cognitive Dissonance
Religion Solves Some of Our Anxiety

Does Religion Exist as a Result of Evolution?
Religion Structures a Community
Perhaps Religion is a Side-Effect
The Benefits of Religion
An Ipsos Survey Compares Religious and Not-So-Religious
    Canadians
Three Questions about Your Religiosity
Turning the Results into Four Types of Canadians
The Day-to-Day Benefits of Religion
Non-Believers
Decay of Religiosity in Wealthy Nations

Our Pursuit of Greater Happiness is Being Re-Defined
Increasing Wealth in the Developed World
Our Developed World has Become Much More Complex
Our Modern World is Not Natural
Historical Timeline Through Evolution
We are Losing Sight of What Makes Us Happy
Desire is Not the Path to Happiness
We Seem Trapped by This Comparative Basis of Happiness
Canadians Are Quite Focused on Money
Great Wealth Is Not Providing Great Happiness
We Are on the Wrong Path!
We Have Not Been Prepared to Deal with Wealth
We Are Behaving Like Trees in the Forest

ACKNOWLEDGMENTS

I am a research executive at Ipsos, the global consumer research company. I come by my market research career honestly. I have always liked facts and explanations. There is a comfort in knowing why things are the way they are. Since I have been a market research professional for over 27 years, I suppose it was only a matter of time when I would try to understand what truly leads to greater happiness. I am pleased to share what I have discovered, especially the findings from a unique study conducted by Ipsos among everyday Canadians. In a nutshell, this book is about happiness. It is about our genetic evolution, religion, being charitable, personal wealth, debt, being passionate, sex, health, age, and much more. We need to understand happiness, and what comprises it, because we are on a declining trend. Canadians are becoming less religious, and our country is experiencing a widening social void left by the absence of religion. We need to match the benefits of religion to help create a more civil, caring, and happier country.

I am also a philanthropist; one of the 85% of Canadian adults who gives money annually for charitable and non-profit purposes. Personally donating and volunteering makes me happy. However, through my research I have learned some unsettling facts about Canadian philanthropy. I always believed we were a caring nation, but this is not so evident in our behaviour. This is why the end of this book is disproportionately focused on giving, volunteering, and the sense of warmth and happiness it provides. Charity is part of the happiness equation, and it needs greater attention for a happier and more civil Canada.

Overall, I hope this book and the Canadian study on happiness help you to discover or at least to clarify the right path for greater happiness.

I must add that if this book is judged to be of any value, it is because I am standing on the shoulders of giants. There are a lot of great thinkers and writers, with mind-opening books related to our genetic evolution, about the nature of happiness, about the role of religion in society, and so on. At the end of this book, I list the authors that I found to be useful and insightful. Maybe you will too.

As much as I am a proud Canadian, I must admit that finding Canadian statistics on various sociological trends is not always easy or even possible. In turn, when necessary, I have used American statistics in belief that the patterns are likely not so dissimilar to those in Canada. After all, our economies and cultures are likely more similar than dissimilar. Nonetheless, you can judge whether you feel the sociological trends feel so different. I indicate the sources when presented, and do include many Canadian observations.

It is also important to absolve Ipsos, and all Ipsos people, business units and partners from any responsibilities or liabilities of this book. I have undertaken the challenge of writing it by myself, and I take responsibility of this as a private individual. This is my perspective, and not that of Ipsos.

I hope this book makes you happy!

INTRODUCTION

When I was 13 years old I really scared myself. Not in a physical way, but in very fundamental emotional way. It was late at night, and a few of us were bored, as young teenagers are apt to be. There was nothing worthwhile on TV! Fortunately, it was a beautiful summer evening. We were in Maine, right on the coast. The sky was very dark, without a cloud. There was no urban light.

Situated on the seaside, we faced the vast ocean. The moon had not yet risen. The Milky Way shone brightly overhead. Everything was crystal clear, just very dark. There was barely a distinction between the sea, horizon, and sky. Our world lay vulnerable and naked with neither clouds nor a nice soft blue sky to blanket us. We lay on our backs looking up. The vastness of the universe started to seep into our minds.

I suddenly started to feel very small and insignificant in our vast universe, millions of light years across. We are but a speck in the universe, and I was just one unimportant and insignificant teenager on the face of the earth. At 13 years of age, I was just starting to grasp my individuality, freedoms, and direction in life. I was shocked into realizing I had no clue about why I existed. Where did the universe come from? What is on the outside of the universe? What existed before our universe? Why are we here? What is the point? To this day, I still remember that evening because it fundamentally scared me. Soon after, we went back in to the comfort of a well-lit house, hoping something new was on TV. Perhaps not the right response, but it made me feel better!

It wasn't until much later as an adult that I realized that this feeling is referred to as existential anxiety. This is the uneasy feeling of not having clear answers to the purpose and existence of our own lives. Some experts claim all humans experience this existential anxiety to some degree. Is it possible that because of existential anxiety that humans also have religion? Religion provides answers and it is a part of being happy.

EXISTENTIAL ANXIETY IS WHY RELIGION EXISTS??

Let me put all of the different pieces of the puzzle on the table, and then we can circle back to discuss them. By the end, hopefully the pieces will come nicely together to present an equation for happiness; a Canadian equation, one which is equally relevant for religious believers and non-believers alike.

The pieces of the puzzle:

- Existential anxiety unsettles a lot of people, and leaves many unanswered questions.
- Since our genetic evolution has wired us to pursue happiness, having a religion or belief system helps to mitigate many anxieties. It gives us reason and purpose. It puts our mind at ease. It gives meaning to life. We have had religious beliefs since the beginning of our recorded history. They are found in all cultures of the world.
- Religion is part of who and what we are. It brings some interesting benefits which agnostics need to appreciate.
- But religion is declining in the developed nations of the world, in correlation with a three-fold increase in our wealth since World War II.
- Unfortunately, our pursuit of greater wealth has not worked well for us.
- This does not necessarily mean we need to turn back to being more religious. Religion is not the only path to happiness. Nor does religion own morality to guide people to goodness.
- However, the facts imply we need to find a better path

for greater happiness. Happiness in the Western world is getting off-track. We do not appreciate what truly makes us happy.

- To better understand the characteristics of happiness, we will review the differences between happy people and not-so-happy people.
  - What can we learn from a robust Canadian study of happy people?
  - How does money fit in? What about religion? What about relationships or sex?
  - Are there some secrets? Can we learn from others?
- We will observe that the Canadian equation for happiness is about being 97% true to ourselves,... and 3% giving, reflecting our genetic evolution quite nicely!

Full-time happiness is a fool's pursuit. It is natural to often be dissatisfied. This book does not promise any miracles. But it does expose the facts behind the things which can make us happier.

CHAPTER 1

WIRED TO PURSUE HAPPINESS

"Human happiness is so important, it transcends all other worldly considerations" – Aristotle

WALKING ALONG THE EVOLUTIONARY PATH

Hundreds of thousands a year ago in Africa, a horse was born with a slightly longer neck than others. This slightly defective horse gained by being able to reach higher into the trees to eat the juicy leaves which no other horse could reach. The other horses had to share the lower leaves while our longer-necked horse had access to all the juicy leaves for itself. It ate well, and grew to be a stronger member in the herd. Its strength and health gave it a breeding advantage, and its long-neck genes were passed on. This is genetic evolution in action. With a series of similar little genetic defects, over tens of thousands of years, we arrive today at our modern giraffe.

The core focus of genetic evolution is for genes to repro-duce themselves. Any random genetic mutation which gives the biological organism a benefit will help the organism to sur-vive better. In turn, the organism will be fitter to reproduce and to allow the stronger genes to live on. This is about the survival of the fittest of which most readers are likely well aware.

It is through this passage of time with random genetic de-fects which has led to who we are today. Our modern features are those which have helped us to survive through time.

The study of evolution is a unifying force for many of the medical, biological, and psychological sciences that are related to humans. Evolution explains much about what we do today and why. Why shouldn't genetic evolution apply to Homo Sapiens? We have much in common with many other animals. The new science of DNA proves it. The theory of evolution has stood the test of time. Nothing has proven this wrong.

EVOLUTION HAS WIRED US TO PURSUE HAPPINESS

A core fundamental characteristic of our evolution is the pursuit of happiness. Although some of us feel guilty about pursuing greater happiness, we shouldn't. The pursuit of happiness is a normal evolutionary trait which has served our species well. This has been a key motivator to ensure greater fitness and better survival. Dissatisfaction was and remains a key propellant to act.

We have clearly been rewarded to avoid complacency. The more our ancestors (in the wilderness of Africa) distanced themselves from danger, threats, stress, starvation, loneliness, and so on, the more likely they were to thrive. The more our ancestors accumulated food supplies, strengthened their home base, and nurtured supportive tribes, the more likely they were to live and reproduce.

Conversely, complacency is risky. Unexpected events may suddenly compromise survival. Those who were complacent lost out to those who were better prepared. Our pursuit and drive for greater happiness was an asset to our survival. It meant a greater probability of it.

Happiness also acts as the proverbial light at the end of the tunnel. It makes life worth living. The hope for happier times is often the motivation which keeps us going when faced with adversity. It is the rare person who does not consider their level of happiness, whether to increase or simply to maintain it. The motivation for (greater) happiness is one of the most central elements of our existence.

Defining happiness is a very tricky thing. It is not tangible and it is hard to measure scientifically. It is subjective, in the mind of the beholder. However, the important thing for each of us is that we all know happiness when we are experiencing it. When we are unhappy, we look for ways to improve it.

Daniel Nettle, in his book *Happiness. The Secret Behind Your Smile*, describes happiness as having three levels: Level One is the type of happiness from a temporary short-term emotional response (for example, finding $20 in a pocket of your coat). This is often a short-lived event and might not change the overall evaluation of your busy day. Level Two is more about judging your feelings. This is about stepping back and assessing your overall day, or other more lasting event (Did it go well? Was I happy with what transpired?). Level Three is an even higher more encompassing feeling about one's overall quality of life. This is about fulfilling one's potential, feeling in control of life, and is more than any one small event or any one day. Each of these three levels ebb and flow, interact, and can be in contrast (you can be happy with today, but unhappy with your overall quality of life, in general).

Our Big Brain Causes a Psychological Problem

The single most distinct feature of our species is the proportionate size and nature of our brain. It is unlike that found in any other species, and it has given us a huge advantage. One of the features we possess is the ability to imagine, to wonder, and to contemplate. However, frankly, this has some unsettling side effects for our species. We are able to step back and look at ourselves in the vast universe and to ask "Why?" With our large brains we have developed existential anxiety.

But we have also evolved coping mechanisms to deal with such uncomfortable anxiety (to help make things more comfortable, more happy)...

COGNITIVE DISSONANCE

Our species has benefitted by dealing with uncertainty. Our mind has benefited by having answers at the ready so when a threat, problem, or challenge came along, the mind was better prepared to act. A clear settled mind helped our ancestors detect, be decisive, and react to threats which arose in their environment. If we had unsettled and uncertain minds, we would have been slower to decide, and this could have been life threatening for the 99.9% of our evolution in the wilds of Africa. An indecisive mind might have ended up in the stomach of a predator!

We also see many health benefits from a relaxed, happy mind at peace. We sleep better, have less heart disease, live longer, control our weight better, and enjoy many other functional benefits. Evolution has rewarded healthy, clear minds, and punished those with anxiety, uncertainty, and unhappiness.

Many readers are likely aware of the concept of cognitive dissonance which is when we experience conflicting beliefs, values, and emotions. We do not generally like such conflict. We act to reduce or eliminate such dissonance, often changing or downplaying our beliefs, or searching for an alternate belief to tip our feelings in favour of a more settling view. Sometimes we go as far as to abuse alcohol or drugs, and follow other negative behaviour in search of handling our anxieties and mental discomforts. Regardless, we have evolved by dealing with cognitive dissonance, by finding answers, and changing our thinking to reduce our uncertainty.

RELIGION SOLVES SOME OF OUR ANXIETY

Religion provides answers to many otherwise unsettling questions about our existence, the purpose of life, what happens after death, and so on. It helps provide peace of mind, comfort, and strength. It helps mitigate existential anxiety. Religion also allows us to reduce feelings of guilt by making confessions, and seeking salvation. Many religions promise an afterlife as a means of mitigating the fear of death. In short, religion is a very helpful mechanism. This is one of the evolutionary benefits of religion. This is likely why religion is found in every culture of the world since recorded history. The format of the religion is not so important as long as it helps the believers. It has been helpful to our existence.

In an Ipsos survey among Canadian adults, which I will be highlighting later, I found evidence of this very topic:

- Those who are most religious (believe in a god, practice their religion more often, and claim to be quite religious) do indeed get the emotional benefits of their religion. In the Ipsos survey, 72% agreed with the statement: "In my week-to-week life, I get *comfort and strength* from religion."

- These religious Canadians are also more likely to be "actively seeking more meaning in their life" (39% agree) versus the least religious Canadians (just 23% agree they are seeking meaning). To say this another way, for those seeking meaning, religion seems to help provide the solution. It provides meaning and comfort.

Before our species ever had currency, accumulated wealth, pasteurized food, refrigeration, great medical care, and technological "must haves" (read: microwave ovens, digital TV, various Apple gizmos, PCs, and so on), we had religion. It is one of the first, basic, core elements which helped our species cope and to experience greater peace-of-mind (happiness). This demands a brief review of the benefits of religion in Canada. Religion has been a natural part of the happiness equation ever since we developed our larger brains. This is why religion is so important.

## Chapter 2

Religion's Role

"If God did not exist it would be necessary for us to invent Him." – Voltaire

Does Religion Exist as a Result of Evolution?

The reason for religion is a hotly debated issue. Some suggest that religion is the purpose of life: Humans are to serve the word of their god; a god created the very universe and existence of mankind. Others believe more strongly in the theory of evolution, and feel religion is just one more (quasi) genetic feature of our species. Whether you believe in the science of evolution and/or believe in intelligent design with the creation of mankind by a god, it is rather obvious that the concept of religion exists. This is not a discussion about which one god or religion is true, and this is not a discussion about whether any god actually exists or not. The sheer existence of so many different religions and the belief in so many gods and spiritual leaders makes it rather obvious that our species has accepted, nourished, and benefited from the concept of religion. Just look around to find the evidence of its existence, today, in every culture, and through all of recorded history.

We have religion because it has been beneficial to our species. It does not matter which religion is true. We have simply gained by having a religious or spiritual belief system to help us get through our lives better.

Religion Structures a Community

Beyond comfort and benefits which religion offers its believers, some evolutionists suggest that religion has another evolutionary benefit to our survival. Religion in a community helps to organize and structure the community. A shared belief system helps to bind the tribe. And a strong tribe survives better than a weak or fragmented one. A common religion or belief system, with its rituals and practices allows the group to act in a more homogenous and predictable manner. Clearly, our species has lived in and benefited from being a member of a tribe or community. Religion has contributed to the community's functionality.

PERHAPS RELIGION IS A SIDE-EFFECT

On the other hand, some other evolutionists suggest that religion may be more of an indirect characteristic or random leftover (like our tail bones represent the residual existence of a longer tail found in our ancestral roots): Present, but not so relevant. Perhaps this is true; maybe not. Regardless, this point-of-view does not deny the existence of religion through our evolution, and it does not mitigate the benefits we observe in society (in the Ipsos study).

One thing about genetic evolution is that characteristics which are good for us live on, and those which have been detrimental fade away. To date, religion has not evolved away across the globe, or at least not the *benefits* of religion. What do we find about these benefits?

THE BENEFITS OF RELIGION

This book is not about trying to convert readers to become more religious. However, it is useful to review our many religions to better understand greater happiness. There must be benefits otherwise religion would not have been so supported throughout history, and in all cultures of the world.

Owing to the prevalence of religion, it should come as no surprise that there is a lot of discussion, research, and printed material about the benefits (and costs) of religion. We have already covered the advantages of religion addressing existential anxiety, but there are also many practical day-to-day benefits as many studies suggest:

- Angus Deaton from Princeton University writes in a July 2009 paper about aging, religion, and health that in most countries, religious people report better health; say they have more energy, that their health is better, and that they experience less pain. Their social lives and personal behaviours are also healthier; they are more likely to be married, to have supportive friends, and they are more likely to report being treated with respect. (http://www.princeton.edu/~deaton)

- Research also shows that people with higher religious attendance have a lower risk of death, and live longer. Religious attendance works through increased social ties and behavioral factors to decrease the risks of death. And although the degree of a longer life varies by cause of death, the benefits are consistent across all major causes. (National Health Interview Survey-Multiple Cause of Death; http://www.cdc.gov/nchs/products/elec_prods/subject/mortmcd.htm)

- Wen-Chun Chang also reports on the benefits of religion in Eastern culture. His paper investigates the relationship between religious attendance and subjective well-being in Taiwan. The findings of this study indicate that religious attendance has positive relationships with happiness as well as greater satisfaction with interpersonal relationship, health, and marital life. What is also interesting is that the author did not find a similar benefit based on the satisfaction with personal financial status. (Marburg Journal of Religion: Volume 14, No. 1. May 2009).

- Many other research studies collaborate with these benefits: Religious involvement tends to reduce health-detrimental behaviours and mitigate mental distress associated with physical illness. Religion promotes happiness in people through social cohesion, increased self-esteem and community service. Greater spiritual well-being correlates with less risk of depression. Higher levels of religious attendance were associated with lower risk of depression. (Idler, 1987) (Ferriss, 2002) (Yi, et al, 2004) (Aranda, 2008).

What about Canadians, in our Everyday Lives? What Benefits do we Derive from Religion?

AN IPSOS SURVEY COMPARES RELIGIOUS AND NOT-SO-RELIGIOUS CANADIANS

In June 2010, Ipsos (also known as Ipsos Reid, the largest consumer research firm in Canada) conducted a survey based on an unbiased and randomly representative sample of Canadians, between 18 and 80 years of age. The sample was quite large, comprising over 1,000 independent interviews, across all ages, in English and French, with both males and females. The survey asked Canadians about their happiness, their satisfaction with many different characteristics of their lives, which aspects of their lives they wished to be better, and many personal characteristics which described themselves. A small set of questions asked Canadians how religious they were. Among other things, I wanted to see in which way the more religious Canadians compared to the less religious Canadians.

To be clear, many Canadians are not so religious, but there is also a segment which is quite religious. To make our analysis simple, we split our respondents into four groups, ranging from the most religious and observant, to the least religious (agnostic/atheist). Can we learn something about the benefits of religion across our four groups of everyday Canadians?

Perhaps you would like to see how you compare? The following page outlines the three questions used in the Ipsos poll to classify Canadians by their religiosity...

THREE QUESTIONS ABOUT YOUR RELIGIOSITY...

Q.1) In terms of religion, religious beliefs, and practicing religious behaviour, how religious do you feel you are? The **more** religious you feel you are, score closer to **10**, The **less** religious you feel you are, score closer to **1**

How religious?

Not at all religious   Quite religious

1	2	3	4	5	6	7	8	9	10
☐	☐	☐	☐	☐	☐	☐	☐	☐	☐

Q.2) How certain are you in your belief in a God? (Respondents were asked to choose one of the three following answers)

Absolutely believe there is a God

Kind of believe there is a God

Do not believe at all in a God

Q. 3) How frequently do you attend religious services, **excluding** weddings and funerals?

Every day

Every couple of days

About once a week

About two to three times a month

About once a month

About four to ten times a year

Just a few times a year (1 to 3 times)

Less often than once a year

Never attend religious services

(excluding weddings and funerals)

Turning the Results into Four Types of Canadians

Based on the results of these three questions, I created four groups to classify Canadians, from the most religious to the least religious...

Most Religious Group: Represents 18% of Canadian adults
Q. (b) they "Absolutely believe there is a God," and
Q. (c) they attend religious services *at least once a month*

Somewhat Religious: Represents 33% of Canadian adults
Q. (b) they "Absolutely believe there is a God" (just like the first group), but
Q. (c) they attend religious services *less than once a month*

Barely Religious: Represents 29% of Canadian adults
Q. (b) they "Kind of believe there is a God."
Q. (c) (It so happens that @75% do not go to church/temple/synagogue)

Not Religious: Represents 17% of Canadian adults
Q. (a) scored 1 for being religious ("Not at all"), and
Q. (b) they "Do not believe in God at all."

Other: 3% of Canadians said they did not believe in God, but still scored themselves as being a little religious. This is interesting because it makes one wonder why they are somewhat religious if they do not believe in God. Are they experiencing other benefits? We will touch on some of this as we proceed.

A note about consumer survey results: Any survey among a sample of Canadians has something called sample error. That is, the specific results reported in the study may not be exactly reflective of the total population. This is because the sample may not be perfectly representative, and could be "off" by a little. The larger the sample in the survey, the more likely the sample becomes representative of the total population. In this Ipsos survey conducted for this book, the error range is +/- 3% points on the sample of 1,000 people. This means that any result reported from this survey is likely to be within three points of the real measure in the total population. If this same study was conducted 20 times, then we would expect each study to show the same results, +/- 3%, 19 out of the 20 studies. This is what is called the "margin of error," with 95% confidence. Now you know!

THE DAY-TO-DAY BENEFITS OF RELIGION

True to our genetic evolution, and the prevalence of religion throughout the recorded history of mankind, we indeed find benefits of being religious within this study of everyday Canadians.

These are some of the characteristics people enjoy from being religious...

- Enjoy feeling greater self-esteem,
- Have lower stress,
- Have more time and better relationships with family and friends,
- Have better mental health,
- Are happier in their marital status
- Feel more connected and accepted
- Have support when sick, and people to confide in
- Are more comfortable and accept their appearance,
- And, overall, rate their quality of life higher than the rest of how Canadians rate their respective quality of life.

The following two charts (next page) share some attributes from the survey in which the "most religious" scored much better than the "least religious." These are just some of the advantages of being religious...

BENEFITS OF RELIGION

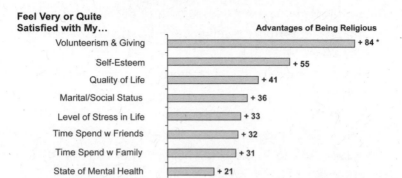

Feel Very or Quite Satisfied with My...

Advantages of Being Religious

Volunteerism & Giving	+ 84 *
Self-Esteem	+ 55
Quality of Life	+ 41
Marital/Social Status	+ 36
Level of Stress in Life	+ 33
Time Spend w Friends	+ 32
Time Spend w Family	+ 31
State of Mental Health	+ 21

#s are Index of Results for "Most Religious" indexed to "Least Religious"

* How to Read: The most religious Canadians scored "Volunteerism & Giving" 1.84 times or 84% higher than the least religious Canadians.

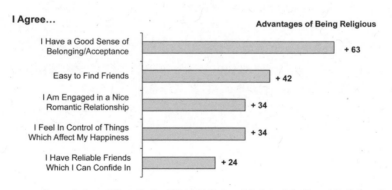

I Agree...

Advantages of Being Religious

I Have a Good Sense of Belonging/Acceptance	+ 63
Easy to Find Friends	+ 42
I Am Engaged in a Nice Romantic Relationship	+ 34
I Feel In Control of Things Which Affect My Happiness	+ 34
I Have Reliable Friends Which I Can Confide In	+ 24

#s are Index of Results for "Most Religious" indexed to "Least Religious"

Source: Ipsos Survey of Canadian Adults, June 2010

In short, religion correlates with better satisfaction in life, and this is the evolutionary benefit which likely explains why religion has been so prevalent throughout our history, in all cultures of the world. Religious Canadians clearly feel more satisfied and happier than agnostics and atheists. Religion has been one of the elements of our *happiness equation*. However, this is changing...

NON-BELIEVERS...

Despite the benefits which religion offers our species, it has also led to a lot of wars, personal persecutions, hatred, intolerance, corruption, abuse, and the list goes on. It is also very costly to an individual to believe in and support a religion. A lot of time, energy, and money is put into being religious each week. Perhaps it is for some of these reasons that people have chosen to be non-believers in the religion of their family or community.

Choosing to be a non-believer does not make a person any better or worse than being a Christian, a Jew, a Muslim, a Buddhist, or whatever. No religion owns morality to define what is good or bad. What is right in the practice of Islam in many countries may not be so consistent with what is right in Christianity. Clearly a non-believer can be a good person in society just like a religious person can be a criminal. Many acts of kindness have been done by non-believers.

DECAY OF RELIGIOSITY IN WEALTHY NATIONS

Perhaps it is for these reasons, in part, that religious observance has been declining in many developed nations. The number of people belonging to a church, temple, or synagogue has been declining on a per capita basis in many of the world's wealthiest nations. Why? There is a direct inverse correlation between the religiosity of a nation versus its standard of living in a nation and its level of education. Most of the wealthy nations now offer greater health care, good access to education, strong social security and welfare services, tax-advantageous retirement savings plans, and overall, provide safe, easy living conditions. Perhaps citizens in wealthy nations do not need or do not derive the same benefits from religion? Perhaps they are less anxious, and in less need of the comforts offered by religion? Furthermore, education has allowed many to independently develop their own belief systems.

This decline in religiosity in the wealthiest nations is being felt in the churches, synagogues, and temples. *And some interesting consequences are being felt in our daily lives.*

(Hopefully you will come to see that this debate about evolution, religion, and the existence of a god is not what matters. This argument is starting to get stale. Neither side will win. Evolution is about science while religion is about beliefs. The two do not meet! I feel it is much more relevant to understand what makes us happy since this is a core motivation for our existence. Happiness motivates us, whether through religion, or not. Religion is just part of the happiness equation. Another important consideration is money...)

CHAPTER 3

In Pursuit of Happiness Through Wealth

"When it's a question of money, everybody is of the same religion." – Voltaire

Our Pursuit for Greater Happiness is Being Re-Defined

After millennia of slow genetic evolution, our pace of change has picked up speed. And it seems to be hitting a speed bump. In the past 100 years, life in the developed nations has created a society which barely relates to the world which dictated our evolution. Excess and riches have replaced scarcity. Our "tribes" are much bigger than in the past (containing so many strangers). Our life is becoming very complex due to technology and the range of choices it opens to us. Medicine has doubled our life expectancy without a chance for our biological evolution to adapt. Our natural outdoors have been replaced by concrete. We spend 90% of our time in-doors in mechanical worlds out of touch with the natural rhythms of nature.

Increasing Wealth in the Developed World

In the past 100 years, there has been a significant growth in wealth. The scope of this wealth is unprecedented in our evolutionary history. A quick review of the GDP in the USA over the past 100 years (in constant dollars, i.e. adjusted for inflation) illustrates the real increase in greater wealth. The Canadian situation is similar.

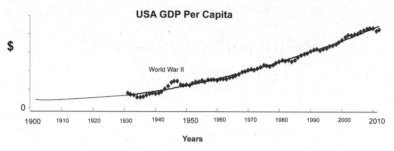

Source: US Department of Commerce, US Bureau of the Census

Our Developed World has Become
Much More Complex

Along with greater wealth, we have also developed much more complexity of choice. For the longest time, our ancestors had simple decisions: Where to sleep, what to eat, and so on. In turn, our survival did not require the ability to process many complicated tasks. However, this has changed quickly for our species. In the last 100 years, our environment has provided much more complexity, with much choice. We can choose to eat almost any ethnic food, watch over 100 television stations, travel to almost anywhere in the world, surf millions of Internet websites, and so on. Our commercialism provides a plethora of choice. The rate of technological advancement is faster than ever before. Previously, our brains never had to deal with such change, complexity and choice. Many of our decisions are now so complex we struggle to cope with all of the elements.

As we find ourselves in this new world, we do not really appreciate what truly makes us happy. And many of us do not appreciate what comprised our happiness through 99.9% of our evolution. It is as if our genetic evolution barely applies... We are without a proper user manual. We do not have the benefit of evolutionary experience. *We are not well equipped to deal with this explosion of wealth and complexity... And it shows!*

Our Modern World is Not Natural

As much as evolution explains who we are, we also need to recognize that over 99.9% of our genetic evolution (millions of years) has been in the wild, on the plains of Africa. This is the world we evolved in. Today's world is nothing like the environment which shaped us. The past two centuries of our history is just a short blip in time. It is not long enough to allow our species to evolve well for our very different modern world. In the following chart, we can see how recent our modern civilized world represents in our evolution. If we go back only to the beginning of primates, we have a 40-million-year evolutionary path. For over 40 million years we had a slow gradual evolutionary path, in a slowly changing environment...

Historical Timeline Through Evolution

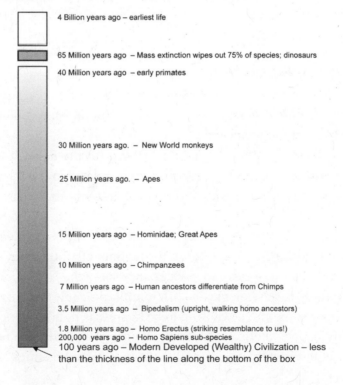

4 Billion years ago – earliest life

65 Million years ago – Mass extinction wipes out 75% of species; dinosaurs

40 Million years ago – early primates

30 Million years ago. – New World monkeys

25 Million years ago. – Apes

15 Million years ago – Hominidae; Great Apes

10 Million years ago – Chimpanzees

7 Million years ago – Human ancestors differentiate from Chimps

3.5 Million years ago – Bipedalism (upright, walking homo ancestors)

1.8 Million years ago – Homo Erectus (striking resemblance to us!)
200,000 years ago – Homo Sapiens sub-species
100 years ago – Modern Developed (Wealthy) Civilization – less than the thickness of the line along the bottom of the box

The rate of change in our world, fueled by amazing technological and medical advances, has increased to a pace much faster than we can keep up with through biological evolution. To best understand our current human characteristics, it helps to keep in mind a picture of life in the wild plains of Africa! *The developed world we suddenly find ourselves in is nothing like that which made us what we are today.*

WE ARE LOSING SIGHT OF WHAT MAKES US HAPPY

Today, most people fail to recognize what comprised our happiness outdoors in nature, with close tribal ties, face-to-face communication, contributing to the tribe, helping others, and earning mutual support in return, all without much wealth. Today, instead, many have placed their focus on money, and in the promise it is supposed to afford. *Money has become the criterion behind many of life's decisions (in misplaced hope it yields greater happiness).*

DESIRE IS NOT THE PATH TO HAPPINESS

Since we are so occupied with happiness, it is relevant to recognize the difference between *desire* and *happiness*. These are two different concepts:

- The concept of *desiring* something (in the belief it will make us happier) is more strongly related to the release and function of dopamine in the brain (in the "pleasure centre").
- On the other hand, *happiness* is more closely related to the function of serotonin throughout all of the body.

To make this clear so we can appreciate the importance, happiness is physiologically different than simply wanting or desiring something. Wanting to be happier is not the same as being happy. There are different things going on in our bodies...with different effects on how long the good feelings last, and different effects on our health.

The concept of desire has been a hugely important concept throughout our evolution. As discussed earlier, it has been the motivation and propellant to act in favour of greater survival fitness. However, how we become happy through desire is not so straightforward....

- At the minimalist end of the spectrum, our desire is focused on the necessities of survival. *These are judged in absolute:* Do I have enough food and water to sustain my life? Am I warm? Am I safe from danger? For those familiar with Maslow's Hierarchy of Needs, it is the first level. For the vast majority of our evolution, this is what occupied much of our attention. We rarely got past level one.

- Once life surpasses the basic threshold level of survival, and then escalates to levels well above survival, happiness becomes more *comparative*. We change from judging happiness in absolute, and replace it by judging happiness on a comparative basis. We judge our happiness by comparing what others are accomplishing or have. The happiness with my television is judged in comparison to other people's TVs. The television which we are very satisfied with today may be quite unacceptable if everyone else has a better one next year! Life becomes a case of "keeping up with the Jones."

This comparative basis for judging happiness is relatively new to our species. We have never been so far above our survival threshold in our evolutionary history to change so fundamentally from an absolute judgment to this new comparative judgment of happiness. In turn, we are losing touch with the absolute nature of being happy. *Today, our "wants" have replaced our "needs."* We act as if wanting and getting things will make us happier. Somehow happiness has become a competition with our neighbours. In hindsight, we know this is not the case. We need to remind ourselves that overall happiness is better related to serotonin, and the characteristics which lead to a healthy level, and not related to the short term hit of dopamine from wanting and getting something.

We Seem Trapped by this Comparative Basis of Happiness

Through evolution, life always had a certain level of competitiveness. Within our ancestral tribes, like most social animals, there was always a competition for scarce resources, to dictate who mates with whom, who eats first on the latest kill, who sleeps in the best spot, who acts as "lookout," and so on. It was not a useful situation to be disadvantaged versus others in the tribe. Thus, comparing and competing has always been prevalent. But recently, in the developed world, this evolutionary concept of tribal competitiveness has become quite irrelevant because our tribes are all so far above the survival threshold. Not having the best TV in the community is really not so life-threatening! It is mostly because we find our species in this new and very rare situation of extreme wealth, so high above the survival threshold that our comparative nature seems so ill-conceived and inappropriate in this new environment.

Since so many of us have our happiness influenced by *comparative evaluations* to others, we seem destined to never get ahead and stay ahead. In turn, we do not get collectively happier as a society because we are no longer judging happiness in absolute. But enough already! We can now recognize that we are well beyond the survival threshold. *We need to learn that our evolution is now failing us because we have never been in such a position of accumulated wealth.* We need to appreciate the inappropriateness of judging our happiness by comparing to our neighbours. And the fact is (as we will see later in a few pages) that by accumulating more wealth we are not becoming happier in the Western world.

Canadians Are Quite Focused on Money

Focusing on money is easy to understand. It is easy for us to measure. However, we constantly fail to translate the benefits of this money. We can appreciate that by working harder, we can earn more. But we are poor at understanding the utility of this extra money versus the cost of earning it. Since we are poor at anticipating how we will feel in the future, we naively believe that collecting greater wealth will provide us greater happiness. Ironically, for many of us, the extra burden of working harder is becoming disproportionately more than the benefit we derive from doing so.

From the Ipsos survey of Canadian adults we can see how important money is to our motivations...

- 62% of Canadians think *every week* about the amount of money they are earning.
- Just 25% are quite or very satisfied with their financial position.
- 59% want more money than happiness in their life.
- 63% say having more money in their life is very or quite desired.
- *"Wanting more money" scored higher than wanting more personal time, less stress, more friends, more sex, better physical appearance, or having a better marriage!*

From Industry Canada we learn...

- Since 1984 our personal debt load has more than doubled (per family). Although debt alone does not provide a full picture because our assets (mostly, the value of our homes) have also increased, the debt-to-assets ratio has indeed increased.

- Our ability to pay our debts is weakening, and we are spiraling out of control: The debt-to-income ratio has increased from 74% to over 100% (from 1989 to 2008).
- And our savings rate has dropped from 14.1% in 1989 to less than 2%.

In the USA, and perhaps not so different in Canada, the bankruptcy rate per capita has quadrupled since 1985 (Source: US Federal Reserve Board).

Here we are in the developed nations, beyond our genetic evolutionary comfort zone, moving away from the benefits of religion, in pursuit of greater wealth, to sate our wants. It raises a logical question: "Is this working for us?" Are we actually happy?

GREAT WEALTH IS NOT PROVIDING GREAT HAPPINESS

So much wealth has been created in the Western nations in the past 50 years. The USA is a very wealthy nation, with perhaps the greatest freedoms and one of the strongest democracies in the world. Despite all of this, the level of happiness in the USA has not increased over the past many decades, and nor is the USA one of the happiest nations...

The "World Values Survey" led by Ronald Inglehart (University of Michigan), aims to measure peoples' happiness and life satisfaction across many nations. It asks just two basic questions: "How would you rate your happiness?" and "How satisfied are you with your life these days?" It has compiled data from 350,000 people in 97 countries since 1981. So who is the happiest in the latest wave (2006-2008; www.worldvaluessurvey.org)?

- Denmark ranks number one.
- Puerto Rico and Columbia rank number two and three, despite having noticeably *lower* GDP per capita.
- Canada ranked ninth.

- **The USA ranks only 16th for happiness.**

The American "General Social Survey" (www.norc.org/ GSS+Website) which conducts basic scientific research on the structure and development of American society reports that "happiness" in the USA has been declining since the early 1970s to date. This is similar to another poll in the UK. In a gfk NOP poll for the "Happiness Formula" TV series on the BBC in the UK, the proportion of "very happy" Brits has fallen from 52% in 1957 to 36% in 2005.

In a recent 2009 report from the Organization for Economic Co-Operation and Development (based in Paris), happiness levels are highest in northern European countries, which are more socialistic in their approach to life. Canada, which also has a relatively socialistic society, ranked sixth. The USA did not make the top 10 nations.

It is worth a pause to realize the implications – Why is the USA, which is the wealthiest and most free nation in the world not also the happiest? Is this correlated to the decline in religiosity? Is this due to the inadequacies of pursuing wealth? Is the American ideal of liberty over civility an ill-advised value?

WE ARE ON THE WRONG PATH!

Are Westerners on the wrong path? Along with the growth in wealth, here are a few North American trends over the past 50 years for you to consider:

- Work life has taken more of our time each day. (Source: A. McFarlane & L. Tedds, University of Manitoba, July 2007 – www.mpra.ub.uni-muenchen.de)
- The average distance and time commuted to work has increased. (Source: A. McFarlane & L. Tedds, University of Manitoba, July 2007 – www.mpra.ub.uni-muenchen. de)
- Families share fewer meals together. (Source: A. Mc-

Farlane & L. Tedds, University of Manitoba, July 2007 – www.mpra.ub.uni-muenchen.de)

- We spend less time on meals. (Source: A. McFarlane & L. Tedds, University of Manitoba, July 2007 – www.mpra.ub.uni-muenchen.de)
- We are also spending less time on personal care. (Source: A. McFarlane & L. Tedds, University of Manitoba, July 2007 – www.mpra.ub.uni-muenchen.de)
- Obesity is a growing problem. (Source: Centers for Disease Control and Prevention, US Department of Health and Human Services.)
- Membership in clubs and community organizations has declined. (Source: http://www.infed.org/biblio/social_capital.htm)
- On average, we have less than three close friends. This number is declining. (Source: June 2006 issue of the journal American Sociological Review)
- Americans entertain friends at home less often. (Source: http://www.infed.org/biblio/social_capital.htm)
- Trust between Americans has declined. (Source: http://www.infed.org/biblio/social_capital.htm)
- There is 40% decline in the empathy of university students towards others, versus 1980. (Source: May 2010 Annual Meeting of Association for Psychological Science)
- We pass a greater amount of time alone, with the TV and/or on the computer. (Source: Nielsen's "Three Screen Report")
- Divorce rates have increased, and the USA has one of the highest rates anywhere. (Source: http://www.divorcerate.org/)

I think most readers will conclude that these above trends are depressing. Our pursuit of money and the actual accumulation of greater wealth have not led to greater happiness. We are very poor in translating the utility of money to happiness and to our feelings. *We have lost the historical evolutionary path for (greater) happiness.*

We Have Not Been Prepared To Deal with Wealth

For hundreds of thousands of years, we never accumulated and stored wealth. Our ancestors did not have access to refrigeration, pasteurized food, or the means to keep significant food supplies. They had no currency or other forms of saving meaningful assets. In short, our evolution has not comprised the concept of *accumulated* wealth beyond what we needed to survive in the short term. Only recently has the average Westerner had a constant and secure access to food, water, and shelter without having to struggle for it daily.

Today, in the wealthiest nations where we have more wealth than needed, we find that old "habits" die hard. We may not really *need* so many things for our survival, but we are still wired to pursue happiness through (greater) wealth. For all of our evolution we pursued "assets" for our survival. This genetic instinct cannot be turned off or ignored so quickly. It is in our genes despite no longer being so required. Today, our species is ill-equipped in our strange developed (wealthy) world. It is only very recently that we are living in an environment well above the threshold of scarcity, hunger, and danger.

We find ourselves pursuing happiness in ways we have never practised before in our genetic evolution. We do not know how to best adapt today when we are so far above the required threshold of survival. We are not doing so well in this new situation.

We Are Behaving Like Trees in the Forest

I do not mean to insult the trees, but here is how trees act: Each tree is growing to reach the sun, stretching higher than the others for more sunshine. Over time, all of the trees grow taller and taller trying to compete and outperform the others. So much energy and resources go into the growth of the trees, but they never get ahead or win. The upper canopy just gets higher and higher. The smart strategy would be for all trees to cooperate by growing just a nominal amount, and stop wasting energy and resources for such little net gain. Unlike trees, humans have a brain and can understand the futility! We can design our future strategy. But we are not paying attention. Collectively, we seem to compete to be ever wealthier. So many government policies in the Western nations are geared to creating, supporting or promoting greater wealth, and not more happiness. Unfortunately, like the trees, we are not gaining the advantage of greater happiness. *Surely we are smarter than the trees!*

WE ARE POOR LISTENERS

This discussion about pursuing wealth as the path to happiness is neither new nor unique to the evolutionists. Many of the more popular religions found across the globe have preached against the pursuit of wealth since their inceptions thousands of years ago. A (very) brief review of the most popular religions all appear to support a common concern about accumulated wealth.

Christianity: The Ten Commandments are recognized as the moral foundation of Christianity, and Judaism, and also figure substantiality in Islam. Members are taught to love others, avoid stealing, and to not covet. Christianity teaches generousity, kindness to others, and charity.

Judaism teaches that a person's worth is unrelated to his wealth. Wealth is a responsibility to be used to benefit the poor and to advance religious studies.

Islam: Islamic economics discourages hoarding of wealth,

unbalanced business practices, and charging or earning interest on wealth.

Buddhism: The Four Noble Truths teach about the suffering caused by craving. Suffering ends when craving ends.

Hinduism perceives that the material world is not the real world. Members should free themselves of self-centredness, cruelty, greed, and other vices.

Sikhism: One of the main pillars of Sikhism is to share wealth (to give whatever possible away to the community). Wealth is unimportant.

The point is this: For thousands of years our societies have been taught about moderation, and the ills of accumulating wealth. However, this message is being lost as developed nations become less religious. With the advancement of technology, medical advancement, mass marketing, and commercialism, we are struggling. With less and less people attending religious services, and being less observant, the wisdom of religion is passing unheeded.

Our Big Brain Is Mostly to Blame for Our Problems

For almost all animals, and for most of our genetic evolution, our stress system served us well. When challenged by a threat (a predator in the wild of Africa) our body responded quickly by releasing adrenalin leading to an accelerated heart rate, higher blood pressure, expanded blood vessels, and heightened senses. This equipped us to act quickly to better preserve life: to fight or flee. However, this stressed state is costly and not healthy when sustained over long periods of time. This is the idea behind Robert Sapolsky's book *Why Zebras Don't Get Ulcers*.

Sapolsky is a Stanford University neuroscientist who has spent decades studying primates. He argues that many social animals (like the zebra living in its herds) don't have very complex emotional systems, or big brains. They also spend a lot of time of each day acquiring the food they need to survive. Zebras have little time and little brain power to think or to imagine. On the other hand, thanks to the power of our brains (technology and medicine), humans in developed nations no longer need to constantly worry about food and survival from day to day. We have manipulated our world to our (short-term) advantage. In turn, we have many hours of free time each day to pre-occupy our minds with other things beyond survival. With more free time, and a bigger brain, humans have developed psychological stress and depression. This is a side effect which has developed along with a bigger brain. Humans epitomize this mental stress more than any other species, thanks to our much larger brain.

Our Biological System is Not Coping

This psychological stress is where our biological systems are letting us down. For millennia, our stress response system worked in relatively short intense bursts (to flee or fight). Our survival depended on it. Only recently have we created a new environment in the developed world unlike anything we lived in before. We have created a situation with so much time to create constant psychological stress, sustained over long periods of time. Our careers, finances, the density of people, our manipulated environment, complexity of choices, social structures, and so on, are new to us. We were never equipped to deal with such an environment. Many Westerners now live with sustained stress causing heart disease, adult-onset diabetes, weakened immune systems, and other health-threatening problems. *Our brains have led us down a path for which we are genetically ill-equipped.*

Sapolsky has found that baboons in the wild have a similar problem. Wild baboons in Africa have few serious dangers, and have a lot of free time. They have also developed complex social structures in their troops. Sapolsky has found stress and high levels of stress hormones (in blood samples) from many baboons. Even when not in life-threatening situations, many baboons live with a heightened level of stress as a consequence of their social structure and non-life-threatening stressors. The problem with humans is that our world has evolved a lot further than that of our primate cousins, and very rapidly in the last few 100 years. In turn, our bodies are showing signs of these sustained levels of stress for which we are not equipped to handle. We need to learn what is causing our stress, and relieve the causes to find greater happiness. Our life and health depend on it.

CHAPTER 4

SO, HOW SHOULD WE PURSUE HAPPINESS?

"Most people are about as happy as they make up their minds to be." – Abraham Lincoln

OUR MOTIVATION FOR HAPPINESS IS BEYOND ITS SURVIVAL BENEFIT

Just as it is for most animals today, happiness for humans used to be quite simple. Happiness was primarily the absence of sadness. That is, when our mind was at peace, we were happy. If we were not starving, not under threat from a predator, and not in any other danger, we were happy. If we were not cold or wet, we were happy. If we had a secure tribe, personal connections, and with others to help look after us, we were happy. In a sense, this was as good as it got. There were no materialistic goods to worry about or covet. *Life was not about accumulating "positives," but rather it was largely about avoiding "negatives."* Unfortunately, through history, we rarely had the chance to be complacent because life was a constant struggle. Life was tough. It has only been our very recent history which has provided so many material comforts, advances in medicine, food preservation, and so on.

Of the core emotions which humans have developed, as a consequence of our evolution, most are negative emotions: fear, anger, disgust, grief, surprise, and so on. On the positive side, we have joy. This bias to negative emotions is what equipped us to thrive. It was sufficient to our survival, mostly because negative situations are more life threatening than positive ones! Joy and related positive emotions were not as important as a survival response. Emotions were mostly developed from negative experiences. Happiness was simply the absence of these negatives.

Even as modern humans started to live in communities 15,000 years ago, our ancestors had to continue to work long hard days, for minimal food. Disease was a problem, war and violence was constant, and human rights were basically non-existent. Only in the last 60 years since World War II have we advanced so much that we now find ourselves in a world where our evolutionary concept of happiness has become somewhat irrelevant. This is the first time (the first full generation) in over 40 million years since the emergence of primate evolution that we are so far above the survival threshold in the Western world. We are now significantly removed from the life-threatening stressors which defined our level of sadness and fear.

Happiness is NOT About Being Rich

A review of nations around the world shows us that as wealth increases, happiness also increases. However, this is only mostly true at the low end of the wealth spectrum. The poorest nations are generally the least happy. Once a certain threshold of wealth is achieved, greater happiness starts to depend less on greater wealth.

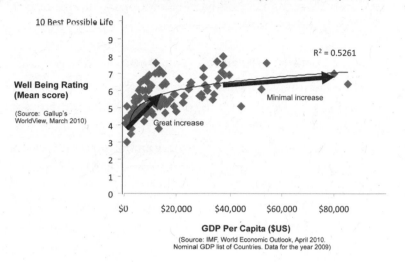

Countries Across the World: Happiness X $GDP per capita

10 Best Possible Life

$R^2 = 0.5261$

Well Being Rating
(Mean score)

(Source: Gallup's
WorldView, March 2010)

Minimal increase

Great increase

GDP Per Capita ($US)
(Source: IMF, World Economic Outlook, April 2010.
Nominal GDP list of Countries. Data for the year 2009)

I think the right way to understand this is that the lack of wealth in the poorest nations really reflects the absence of basic human needs such as food, clean water, safe shelter, sanitary conditions, and basic medial care for survival. Once a nation's wealth surpasses the level where basic human needs are met, greater wealth starts to reflect a different focus for happiness.

Once the level of sadness and misery are surpassed, what becomes the nature of happiness? In large part, the focus turns to accumulating wealth (and the things it affords). *And it is because accumulated wealth is so rare and so new to our species that we are not well equipped to judge it, deal with the implications, and understand the cost of obtaining it.* In turn, more (accumulated) wealth stops creating greater happiness.

However, unlike other species (and being smarter than the trees!), we have the ability to learn, adapt, and adjust our lives to focus on what indeed makes us happier. We can compromise and make the necessary trade-offs. However, we first need to truly recognize the basic evolutionary nature of our happiness, and what it is to be human.

WE HAVE CERTAINLY IMPROVED OUR STANDARD OF LIVING

Here are a few things we have gained in North America over the past 50 years. Although this is US data, we are not likely so dissimilar in Canada.

- The median size of a new American house has increased over 50% since 1970. (Source: National Association of Home Builders; March 2006)
- And over 75% of these homes now have air conditioning. (Source: US Energy Information Administration, June 2010)
- With over 85% equipped with a microwave oven. (Source: US Energy Information Administration, June 2010)
- About 85% have computers, and over 75% have home access to the Internet. (Source: US Energy Information Administration, June 2010)
- 95+% have colour televisions, 80% with two or more, and 35% have large-screen TVs. (Source: US Energy Information Administration, June 2010)
- 90+% have VCRs or DVRs. (Source: US Energy Information Administration, June 2010)
- And over half of homes have two or more cars. (Source: US Census Bureau, Sept 2008)

The point is we have added a lot of luxury into our lives in the past 50 years. One might think it would have made us happier. But we know that "happiness" has not increased, and has more likely decreased (depending on which study you read).

We need to learn that materialistic things (such as the

things in the above list) do not actually make us fundamentally happier!

We Are Poor Judges of Our Future Happiness

As a consequence of our big brains, we have the capacity to imagine, wonder, dream, and to consider our future. We can plan ahead with a certain amount of control in an attempt to achieve our preferences and to achieve greater happiness. This is our big brain at work. However, we are far from perfect at planning ahead. We are not so good at imagining our future feelings. We lack the realism. We are not capable of foreseeing everything we need, and judging the costs and benefits of each choice. In the absence of perfect information, we imagine and creatively fill in the gaps for what is missing. When judging future events, we are often biased by how we feel in the current moment. We downplay certain elements, over-estimate others, and get clouded by our desires. We also often rely on past experiences, but fail to appreciate that our memories have biased those perspectives as well. In short, despite our big brains we are not smart enough to forecast well our future feelings!

Imagine choosing a place to go in your town for a pizza and glass of red wine or cold beer. Go ahead and picture it now....

It is likely that what you imagined and what you will ultimately experience will not be exactly aligned. Many things which you failed to imagine will influence you (the cheese on the pizza was not quite what you envisioned, the crust was thicker or thinner than you wanted, the time you had to wait for the bill to arrive was too long, the washrooms at the restaurant were not what you expected, the temperature of the restaurant was too cool or too warm, the lighting was too light or too dark, the noise level was too loud, the desserts were great or perhaps not so good, the temperature of the coffee, the traffic getting home from the restaurant, or whatever). Most of these elements were not necessarily assessed when you were considering your choice. There is a very good chance you did not evaluate all of the very things which, in hindsight, will influence your happiness. This simply reflects our inability to properly and realistically judge the future. And this is just for a pizza! How good are we at judging the extra required effort to earn more money, the social implications, and the expected happiness it is supposed to offer?

Daniel Gilbert, in his interesting book *Stumbling into Happiness* suggests that in order for us to judge future anticipated feelings we should talk with others who have already experienced it. If you are planning travel to an exotic destination, to retire, or to move to a new neighbourhood, do not guess at how you might feel; ask someone who has already experienced it. The problem as Gilbert points out, is we tend to naively dismiss the advice of others as not being so applicable (because no one else is just like me; I am different). In short, we do not realize or like to admit that we are poor judges of future emotional experiences. I suppose this is self evident by our lack of progress towards our greater happiness!

John Stuart Mill, the utilitarian philosopher of the nineteenth century, talked about the Hedonic Paradox. This is the notion that by pursuing happiness itself, one makes it more difficult to find. Happiness is found indirectly by pursuing other more meaningful things.

CAN WE LEARN TO BE HAPPIER?

In general, Canadians are quite happy. Indeed, the research shows that most of our species is quite happy around the world. I imagine that this is a necessity otherwise our species may not have had the motivation and wherewithal to evolve forward. Nonetheless, 68% of Canadians think about their level of happiness weekly, and 41% of Canadians actually want more happiness than more money. This raises the question about whether it is possible to become happier. And if yes, do we know what will give us greater happiness? And then, are we able to properly judge the "cost" of pursuing it?

It is also likely worthwhile to point out that a certain level of unhappiness is normal. Our evolutionary path has led us to be a little dissatisfied which has allowed us to avoid complacency. For our own mental sanity, we should accept a certain level of unhappiness more often as being a normal characteristic. Total happiness is fools' gold.

Some Aspects of Happiness Are Beyond Our Control

Regardless, it is this very point about unhappiness that some psychologists and academics cite as the main reason why we cannot really increase our level of happiness. The argument is that happiness is relative and comparative, and we simply do not stay happy all the time without re-adjusting our benchmark such that we always have more to motivate us. There seems to be some truth in this since the levels of happiness have not increased in many developed nations over the past 60 years since World War II. Despite a wide range of possible reasons for greater happiness, most well developed nations are unchanged in happiness (and some studies indicate a decline).

Other experts also suggest that much of our happiness is genetically inherited from our parents. That is, our temperament and personality are largely determined from birth, of which we have no control.

Another significant element affecting our perceptions of happiness is the culture in which we were born and raised. The wealth, ideals, social values, and circumstances of our environment in which we are born strongly influence us. We develop with a certain level of conformity, and by the time we are old enough to run our own lives, we have been imprinted one way or another. Our basis for judging happiness is defined for us by our upbringing. For most of us, the choice of our childhood home is largely beyond our control.

Good News: Some Aspects
of Happiness Can Be Changed!

Although two elements of happiness seem to be beyond our control; our parents' genes, and the cultural imprinting of our upbringing, there are indeed elements we can affect for greater happiness. All is not lost. We still have some control over the things which can make us happier.

We observe that happiness does change or at least differs by age in the Canadian population. Happiness is affected by the various decisions we make in our life stages. Our decisions indeed have consequences. Such characteristics will be reviewed later in the book.

The most convincing argument that happiness can be controlled is through experimentation. Michael Fordyce is a famous academic with many published books and studies on happiness. In his book *Human Happiness – Its Nature & Its Attainment*, he talks about the "Fourteen Fundamentals" of happiness and how these can be taught to people. His evidence, over time, confirms that unhappy people can adjust to become more like happy people, and in turn, increase their very own level of happiness (versus the time before they adjusted their fundamentals). Here is what Dr. Fordyce writes in Chapter 2:

- "In the years that followed we formally experimented with the "Fourteen Fundamentals" many times. The results, a number of which have received wide professional dissemination in professional journals, continue to confirm our original findings...

- According to the results accumulated to date, all experimental data suggests that these "Fourteen Fundamentals" *do indeed have the ability to help average people become significantly happier.*
- In sum, practically everyone we've studied has been able to become more like happy people (if they wish to), and as they do, they become much happier people!"

In a separate, recently released study, the lead research concluded that genes only account for around 50% of well-being, with external factors accounting for the rest. This was based on a very robust study, over 25 years, from the German Socio-Economic Panel Survey (SOEP). This tracked (among other things) the happiness of more than 60,000 people aged 16 years or older, every year between 1984 and 2008. (http://www.cbc.ca/health/story/2010/10/07/happiness-genetic-psychology.html#ixzz11xEu2Oeb).

This is good news! Since happiness is largely a state of mind, it is relatively inexpensive to become happier. I suppose this should not be such a surprise. The ongoing existence of professional career psychologists implies a certain level of benefit derived from getting a different mental perspective on one's life.

It is also unlikely that our species would have survived if happiness was not responsive to its environment and our actions in it. In short, it seems that some of our happiness is genetic, some of it is circumstantial (due to our up-bringing), and some of it is based on what we can control (but not all of it so easily achieved!).

What are the fourteen fundamentals Dr. Fordyce references? They are:

1) Be more active and keep busy,
2) spend more time socializing,
3) be productive at meaningful work,

4) get better-organized and plan things out,

5) stop worrying,

6) lower your expectations and aspirations,

7) develop positive optimistic thinking,

8) get present-oriented (enjoy the moment),

9) work on a healthy personality,

10) develop an outgoing and social personality,

11) be yourself,

12) eliminate the negative feelings and problems (let go of them),

13) close relationships are the #1 source of happiness, and

14) value happiness.

Wired for Compassion

Despite the selfish nature of genetic evolution, and the guiltless, heartless nature of "survival of the fittest," humans have evolved to develop emotional compassion. The ability to sense and feel empathy towards others has been strongly developed in our species.

We need compassion to help raise our children. Raising a child to maturity requires many years, much energy, and a fair amount of anguish. If we felt no compassion or empathy, we would likely have been lousy absentee parents. We would have abandoned our offspring well before they were self-sufficient. Instead, it is quite the opposite. Parents often make personal sacrifices to provide greater advantages for their children. This is compassion at work.

Compassion has also helped us to survive better in tribes. It helps us to build stronger binds in the tribe. Compassion creates a tribal synergy which helps us to work together, and to defend each other.

OUR BRAIN REWARDS US WHEN WE ARE NICE TO OTHERS

Modern scientists are learning, thanks in part to MRI brain scans, that humans have a pleasure center which releases dopamine when we are being altruistic and compassionate to others. Dopamine is a neurotransmitter which gives us a rewarding feeling of happiness and warmth. It is a "feel good" chemical. Through evolution, humans have acquired this direct biological function which provides a specific reward for being cooperative, and caring. In a sense, this is our bribery for being nice, and it has helped us to thrive, in social tribes.

However it is a little ironic that we need to be compassionate before we like it. Only when we offer meaningful compassionate support, *do we learn* that it makes us feel good to do so. Try telling a young child "it is better to give than to receive." In their experience this is simply not true. Receiving gifts is great. To acquire something for no cost is a good thing. Only as we mature do we learn and feel the emotional benefit of helping others, and being altruistic. Only then do we truly feel it is better to give the perfect gift to a loved one than to receive such a gift. Religion teaches this, but with declining religiosity, we are not learning it so well.

COMPASSION OFFERS A BETTER FEELING OF HAPPINESS

Recent scientific studies have shown a longer lasting feeling of warmth due to the act of giving to someone else rather than keeping the same for ourselves. Elizabeth Dunn, a psychology professor at the University of British Columbia, along with her colleagues, says that people often feel happier by spending money on other people than on themselves. In one experiment, her study included giving $5 or $20 to participants. Half were asked to spend the money on themselves and half were asked to spend the money on someone else. Those who spent the money on others scored their overall happiness level (at the end of the day) higher than the group which spent the money on themselves.

In another study, Dunn and her colleagues assessed the employees at a company in the Boston area just before and after the employees received their profit-sharing bonus. The amounts ranged between $3,000 and $8,000, but it was not so much the amount of money which impacted their levels of happiness, but how they spent the money. Those who spent a higher proportion on other people and/or towards charity reported higher levels of happiness.

LOOKING FOR HAPPINESS AMONG REAL PEOPLE. RELIGION IS NOT A REQUIREMENT

These very features of compassion, altruism, and community involvement comprise most modern religions. These characteristics are some of the very things which have been deteriorating in North America over the past 50 years as society moves away from religion. It is not that religion owns these features. We do not need to become more religious. But we can likely learn something by understanding the correlation with the decline of religion in the Western world and our decline in happiness.

Do we need to believe in a god to be good and to be happy? No. Evolution is not about pursuit of religion. We have evolved characteristics which allow religion to be helpful, but genetic evolution is not about religious beliefs. Religion is not a requirement of evolution. Evolution is about survival of genes.

RELIGION DOES NOT OWN MORALITY OR HAPPINESS

Gregory S. Paul, in the *Journal of Religion and Society* (2005), reported the findings of his study of 17 developed nations. He concluded: "The higher rates of belief in and wor-

ship of a creator correlated with higher rates of homicide, ju-
venile and early mortality, STD infection rates, teen pregnancy
and abortion in the prosperous democracies." Clearly, religion
is not promoting such practices, but nor do we need to feel
that religion owns all the right solutions for happiness.

Despite the benefits we observed among more religious
people (earlier in Chapter 2), there are clearly other characteristics which affect happiness as well.

In Robert Sapolsky's study of baboons, with decades of
data, and a keen interest to understand stress he found that
the degree of *social connectedness* which a baboon experiences
is more important than the *social status* or rank the baboon has
in their troop. Humans can learn from this if we stop to recognize and internalize the concept that happiness is not so
much about our status in our community, but rather is dependent on how we socialize and connect with others in our
community. We can reduce stress by ignoring our status in our
careers, and instead focus on having many good friends, socializing with others, and participating in community associations. Helping others is more helpful in reducing stress than
establishing our own status. This has been the way it was for
99.9% of our evolution.

We need to understand the true nature of what makes us
happy, regardless of religion. A good place to explore happiness is to understand the differences between happy people
and not-so-happy people among everyday Canadians.

CHAPTER 5

HAPPINESS IN CANADA

"It's pretty hard to tell what does bring happiness. Poverty and wealth have both failed."
— Kin Hubbard

IPSOS SURVEY COMPARES HAPPY AND NOT-SO-HAPPY CANADIANS

Despite our previous review of the benefits of religion in our Ipsos study of Canadians, the main focus of our survey was to understand which characteristics are associated with happy people, and which are missing in unhappy people. Religion was just one element, which we have already summarized as correlating with happiness. What else do we find about being happy?

Overall, Canadians' satisfaction with their quality of life, appears to be relatively high: 61% of Canadians score themselves 7 to 10. However, not everyone is happy. Overall, the mean average score on the 10-point scale is 6.6. This gives us room to be happier (as a nation).

This is the question I used in the Ipsos survey if you wish to score yourself...

Q. How well do you like your current quality of life?
 – The **more** favourable, score closer to **10**,
 – The **less** favourable, score closer to **1**.

How well do you like your current quality of life?

Not so much   Extremely

1	2	3	4	5	6	7	8	9	10
☐	☐	☐	☐	☐	☐	☐	☐	☐	☐

To contrast the most happy versus the least happy Canadians I allocated respondents into one of three groups based on how they scored on the one-to-10 scale: The happiest group, a middle group, and the least happy group. The middle group acts as a buffer between the two extremes:

Not so much   Extremely

1	2	3	4	5	6	7	8	9	10
☐	☐	☐	☐	☐	☐	☐	☐	☐	☐

The Least Happy: This group represents 39% of Canadian adults	The Middle Group: This represents 44% of Canadians	The Most Happy: This represents 18% of Canadians

FEATURES AND CHARACTERISTICS
OF THE HAPPIEST CANADIANS

Before exploring the strongest drivers of happiness, let's look at some characteristics. There are several meaningful differences. And as you review these elements, you will likely get a sense that some of them are inter-related:

1) **Religiosity** correlates with happiness (as we discussed previously). People who are more religious are also happier...

Level of Happiness...

	Least	Middle	Most
Quite Religious (scored 8, 9, or 10)	16%	17%	29%*
Believe in God	47%	50%	63%*
Attend religious services weekly	14%	14%	21%

Much higher religiosity

**How to read:* The percentages are to be read down the columns under the respective levels of happiness. For example, among the "Most" group, 29% are quite religious, and separately, 63% believe in a god, while 21% attend religious services weekly. This compares to just 16% in the "Least" group who are quite religious, 47% who believe in a God, and 14% who attend religious services weekly.

Overall, the majority of Canadians do not score themselves as being very religious. On a one-to-10-point scale, less than half (46%) of Canadians scored themselves above five.

One in five Canadians are atheists, or at least claim to not believe in a god of any sort. And those who do believe in a god, most do not attend any religious services with any regularity. Over a third of Canadians never attend religious services of any sort. Point 1: Less religiosity correlates with less happiness.

2) **Good health** plays a strong role in happiness. This is not just a case of being in good mental and physical condition, but also exercising, and maintaining weight control. Happy Canadians exercise, control their weight, and are healthier.

	Level of Happiness...		
	Least	Middle	Most
Physical health is very good	21%	42%	57%
Mental health is very good	38%	69%	89%
Had just one, or no flues in past 2 years	32%	33%	49%
Exercise 3 or more times a week	38%	48%	57%
Overweight by 30 or more pounds	38%	26%	21%
	More overweight		Much healthier

Perhaps better health is an obvious characteristic (who does not want to be in good health?). We have all certainly heard or read the headlines about better health. This simply adds another benefit of being healthy. And these results are not coming from a health professional preaching to us. This is the evidence from fellow Canadians! Fortunately (at least for me who enjoys a nice glass of wine), there is no correlation between abstaining from alcohol and being happy! I checked.

One of the challenges or barriers to greater happiness in Canada is obesity. About half of all adults are not so healthy: 61% are at least 10 pounds overweight, and less than half exercise regularly...

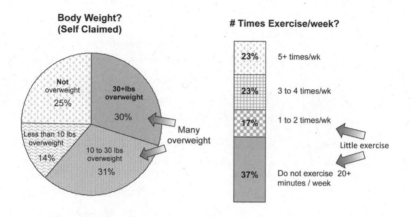

3) The number of hours *working, commuting,* and *sleeping* have **very little** effect on happiness. Is this good news or bad? The trick to happiness is based on the nature and quality of the employment, and what we do in our wakeful time. However, at this point, there is no argument to be made for sleeping more and working less. There is little hope in sleeping our way to greater happiness!

   If the *amount of time* we spend working and sleeping does not affect our happiness, then it is logical to expect that *how* we spend our time does matter...

4) **Less computer and television time.** Those who spend less time on their computer, and/or watching television tend to be a little happier. This is not to say that happy people do not spend a lot of time doing both. The implication seems to be that some unhappy people are spending too much time "on screen." This is also likely inter-related with being

less social, exercising less, loneliness, and other characteristics.

Level of Happiness...

	Least	Middle	Most
Average # hours watch TV per week	17.7	15.9	15.8
Avg. # hrs/wk of personal time on PC	13.8	12.7	12.4
Avg. # hrs/wk socializing (excl. work)	5.8	7.2	8.7

Greater 'screen time' correlates with lower happiness   More socializing

Perhaps the lack of socializing leads to greater amount of
time on the PC or in front of the TV. It is hard to prove which
way the happiness flows. Which is cause and which is effect?
Does the lack of happiness lead to more time with the TV or
PC screen, or is the amount of time spent "on screen" leading
to less happiness? Perhaps it is the latter. One can observe in
the data that interacting with others also correlates with greater
happiness. This implies that trying to have more human interaction produces benefits.

At this point, Canadians tend to spend **much more** time
with their screens (television, computers) than they do socializing with others. Perhaps passing just a few hours less "on
screen" each week would allow us more "face time" with others
to become happier...

	# Hrs of TV %	# Personal Hrs on PC %	Hrs Socializing %
10 or less hours/week	44	59	83
versus 21 or more hours/week	27	15	3

Much more time 'on screen' than socializing

5) **Connecting with others** correlates with greater happiness.
In addition to the above, we see that happy Canadians are
more likely to be members of clubs or associations, volun-

teer more, and have more good friends. Getting out and being a part of the community provides a nice feeling of acceptance.

	Level of Happiness...		
	Least	Middle	Most
A member in 1+ clubs or associations	20%	30%	33%
Volunteer 1 or more hours a month	28%	38%	36%
Avg. # of close personal friends	2.7	3.9	4.0
Feel a good sense of belonging and acceptance in the community	26%	48%	71%
Happy with amount of time with friends	14%	42%	70%
Easy for me to find family or friends to have fun	23%	49%	69%

Joining others is key...
...these are big differences

The people who attend religious services have more friends. The people who volunteer their time have more friends. The people who donate to charity have more friends. The people who exercise more regularly have more friends. I believe the pattern is self-evident. People who get out of the house and engage in their community have more friends. *Happiness is not behind your front door.*

Overall, Canadian adults have, on average, *3.4 close friends.* Only about half of adults claim to have three or more close friends. Characteristics of people with more close friends include: more religious, exercise more regularly, socialize more, less stressed, more charitable, and more memberships in clubs.

6) **More sex please!** Those who scored themselves as being happiest also seem to be more sexually active. Is this a question of the chicken or the egg? I will say no more since I can't prove the direction or causality of this fact. But I do

note that the difference is not so large. Grumpy people are also sexually active!·

Level of Happiness...

	Least	Middle	Most
Sexually active at least weekly	35%	42%	45%
Desire more sex	27%	17%	14%

...There is a slight hint that sex and happiness correlate

I can add two more facts:
- *French Canadians are more sexually active* (52% weekly), versus English Canadians (37%).
- *Sex after 50 declines noticeably* (down to 26% weekly, versus 50% among those *under* 50)!

Frequency of Sexual Activity among Canadian Adults

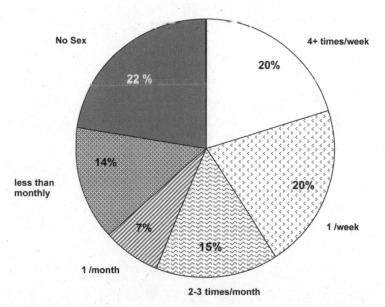

Obviously, one does not need to be married to be sexually active, however, being married does add to the happiness equation...

7) **Marriage** seems to play a strong role in happiness. Those who are married are happier. Those who are single or who have divorced are less happy. Fortunately, many people are married in Canada. But more important than just marriage, *romance* seems to add an extra dividend!

	Level of Happiness...		
	Least	Middle	Most
			Marriage helps...
Currently married	46%	55%	63%
Separated, divorced, widowed	13%	7%	9%
Single	23%	17%	11%
Living together (not married)	18%	21%	17%
Have a nice relationship which is quite *romantic*	29%	50%	71%

...and romance is even better!

Perhaps the correlation of marriage and happiness is similar to some of the other previously mentioned points about connecting with others, socializing, and reflecting our evolutionary roots of being a part of a tribe. There may also be a mental emotional benefit of being married. I say this because those who are *living together*, but are not married, are not happier. There appears to be something more about the institution of marriage.

Do you know which age group is the most romantic? Those in their sixties have a greater incidence of a nice romantic relationship (53% agree) versus any other age group. The youngest adult age group, 18 to 29 years, are the least romantic (36%).

More than age, French Canadians are the most romantic (58%).

Overall, just a little under half of all Canadians enjoy a nice romantic relationship. Hopefully, you are one of them, or can do a few little things to romanticize your life? It is worth a try!

One thing is clear about marriage; happiness does not seem related to having children....

8) **Children** are a lot of work. Although we are often led to believe that having children is fulfilling and offers many happy moments, the facts also indicate that *having children correlates with a less happy time in people's lives*. Children require a lot of energy, sacrifices, and economic costs.

Number of Children (Under 18 yrs) Living at Home...

	None	1	2	3+
Happy; Scored 8 to 10	45%	35%	39%	21%
Sleep 7+ hours week-nights	63%	62%	58%	42%
Exercise 2+ times per week	61%	56%	52%	39%
Socialize 6+ hours per week	44%	37%	37%	27%
Feel in control of my life	37%	30%	31%	21%
I trust people on the street	29%	21%	24%	12%
Happy with my physical appearance	42%	36%	37%	32%
No or little financial debt	52%	37%	33%	29%
# Flues or colds in past 2 years	2.2	3.0	2.8	3.8

Those without children at home seem to have many favourable characteristics!

Sicker

We will also observe later that the least happy time across the age groups is found among those in the child-bearing years. One of the main issues with having the responsibility of young children is the loss of "me time," and the increase in stress...

9) **Stress,** and **being in control**. As we explored in our discussion about baboons and their social stresses, we see that Canadians who are happier have a lot less stress. Manag-

ing stress appears to be a key characteristic towards managing happiness. As we identify and understand what causes our stress, we can then start to manage our lives towards greater happiness.

	Level of Happiness...		
	Least	Middle	Most
Not much stress in life	16%	34%	58%
Happy with the level of stress in life	7%	27%	57%
Feel in good control of life and the things which affect my happiness	11%	39%	74%
Feel trapped in current life situation	37%	8%	5%
Often feel under stress without enough time to accomplish what I want	38%	19%	7%
Stress hurts		A very big infulence	

The *majority* of Canadian adults appear to have an uncomfortable level of stress. Perhaps knowing most other Canadians are also stressed gives us peace-of-mind. To put a fine point on this, we should recognize that the proverbial grass is not really greener on the other side of the fence. We should *not* feel that others are happier, less stressed, and enjoy a better life. It just appears that way because often people put on a brave public face which they rarely enjoy to the same extent in private. Not everyone is happier than you. You are fairly normal if you feel less than averagely happy!

One of the single biggest causes of the stress discussed above is financial in nature...

10) **Financial debt** is a BIG bug-a-boo. Stress and financial debt go hand-in-hand. Those who are least happy are in more debt. They think about money more frequently, and have greater stress. It is not so much one's income level, since this is quite equal across the spectrum of happiness,

but rather it is the lack of financial assets, and having personal debts, which represent the problem. Happy Canadians have much less debt. The least happy Canadians are mostly in debt...

	Level of Happiness...		
	Least	Middle	Most
Annual Income $75,000 or higher	27%	38%	35%
Happy with current financial situation	8%	26%	61%
Have little or no debt	31%	51%	65%
Net Worth $500,000 +	8%	11%	27%
Net Worth Under $25,000	50%	30%	23%
Think about money 2+ times a week	61%	37%	28%
Desire a higher income	49%	30%	19%

Unhappy people are more occupied with money

Happy people have less debt

It is not that one has to be super rich, and have a lot of net worth to be happy. Most Canadians are not super rich! *The trick is to avoid being in debt.*

The big question is how and why did so many Canadians get themselves into such debt? If this was to afford material goods (big house, a second car, a flat screen TV or an air-conditioner during a heat wave) in hope it would bring greater happiness, then this survey suggests that this strategy does not work. This is a real illustration of the macro issues we covered earlier. We observed how the USA has grown in wealth over the past 50 years but failed to boost happiness. This is due, in part, to the significant increase in personal debt levels which Americans have used to buy more than they can afford. And here, in our survey of everyday Canadians, we see living proof that financial debt is a killer of happiness. *The related stress and preoccupation with money is simply not worth the material goods purchased through debt.*

- *35% of Canadian adults have high* (unmanageable) personal debt
- *22% have medium* levels of debt relative to income and assets
- 27% have just a low level debt
- And just 17% of Canadians adults have no financial debt at all.

11) **Doing what you are passionate about.** This one characteristic appears to be more influential than anything else, even more so than monetary issues. The people who know what their strengths are, and spend more time doing what they are good at, and doing what they are passionate about, are really more happy. The differences between the least happy versus the happiest are large.

	Level of Happiness...		
	Least	Middle	Most
Aware of personal strengths	47%	64%	76%
Have opportunity to focus on what good at	18%	38%	65%
Avg. # hrs/wk doing what passionate about	7.5	12.9	17.1
Happy with hobbies, interests, and pastimes	20%	50%	84%

Happiness comes from doing what you are keen about

I found it interesting to explore the characteristics of these Canadians who are doing what they are passionate about because there are *not* a lot of demographic differences to easily distinguish them: They tend to be a little more likely to be retired, and with a slightly lower level of debt (more net worth; but this is likely related to being older). However, there are not many differences by amount of time employed, amount of time commuting, by income, by amount of time sleeping, by sexual activity, and so on.

The trick to unlocking this happiness is to explore and find the things which are engaging to you. To be clear, this is independent of making a lot of money. Those who are spending a lot of time on what they are passionate about have also learned their personal strengths and weaknesses. It appears to me that this is about self-discovery. It is about valuing the benefits of doing things which are interesting and fulfilling. This is about one's hobbies, pastimes, and even interesting employment. *This is about realizing happiness comes from what we do rather than what we earn.*

 # Hours per Week Canadians Spend Doing What Passionate About

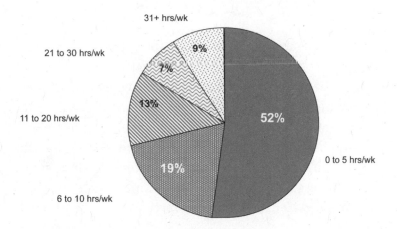

12) **Being charitable.** Some people are passionate about help-
    ing those in need. Others simply do it to reap the rewards
    of meeting new friends, and experiencing a different chal-
    lenge. Perhaps charity also comes with a feeling of duty,
    relief of guilt, and some sense of community. Regardless,
    of the emotional motivation for charity, there is a correla-
    tion between happiness and giving or volunteering. This
    matches earlier discussion about compassion in our
    ancestral tribes, and about our "pleasure centre" in our
    brain when being altruistic. This implies that giving to
    others helps Canadians feel happier.

Level of Happiness...

	Least	Middle	Most
Donated $250 or more in past year	23%	37%	42%
Volunteer 1 or more hours a month	28%	38%	36%
Helping to make my community better	17%	27%	44%

Happiness and giving correlate

Who do you think are more charitable; those who are more
conservative or those who are more liberal?

The answer is that *conservatives* tend to be more charitable.
This is similar in the USA. Conservatives who do not want
government involvement in our lives appear to understand
their own responsibility to help those in need. Those who tend
to believe that governments should be looking after social
welfare are less likely to be charitable. Simply stated, conser-
vative-oriented Canadians are more charitable than liberal-
minded people.

	Most Religious Canadians		Less Religious Canadians	
	Conservative	Liberal	Conservative	Liberal
Donated $500+	38%	28%	21%	21%

Charity and in particular volunteerism adds balance to life (beyond one's income level). It adds a nice change from work life, and offers the opportunity to help others. It offers opportunities to try greater responsibilities and to develop life skills (outside and away from the risk of doing so at your place of work). It is both giving and getting. This concept leads to another characteristic of happy people...

13) **A balanced life.** Happy people tend to experience a greater balance of the many elements of life. This is quite a dramatic observation. The least happy Canadians have practically no balance in their lives (just 8% agree they do).

Level of Happiness...

	Least	Middle	Most
Feel your life is ideally balanced (between work, family, play, exercise, and so on)	8%	36%	69%

Very big difference

Developing a well-rounded life does not mean working less! People who feel their life is well balanced do *not* work less or commute less. The balance comes from including exercise, more socializing, hobbies, and less time "on screen" (the television and/or the computer). In turn, "people in balance" have much less stress and are happier.

Feel Life is Well Balanced...

	Not Balanced	Somewhat	Balanced
# hours **work** per week	21.1	25.6	21.2
# hours **commute** to work per week	2.5	3.1	2.7
# hours **sleep** per week-night	6.8	6.9	7.1
# hours **watch TV** per week	18.1	16.3	15.8
# hours **use a PC** (of personal time) per week	16.1	11.9	12.7
# hours doing what **passionate** about	8.6	11.5	13.9
# hours **socialize** per week	5.1	7.4	7.6
Exercise 2+ times per week	47%	56%	69%
Satisfied with time doing **hobbies, pastimes**	18%	36%	76%

It comes from less time 'on screen', and...   ...from adding non-work elements.

This brings us to the overall big idea of happiness...

14) **Happiness is about perspective.** Happiness is not about money and material assets. Happiness is a perspective on life, about values, authenticity, and sincerity.

Through evolution, happiness came from being connected within the tribe, being loved, and loving others, helping, being healthy, and enjoying the more simple things in life. It was about avoiding sadness. It was not about accumulating wealth (because the concept did not exist!). Happiness is about having the right values and perspective.

The happiest Canadians strongly agree that happiness is a state of mind (79% agree). This is something the least happy Canadians have not all learned (yet).

Level of Happiness...

	Least	Middle	Most
Agree that happiness is a state-of-mind. It is about values.	47%	64%	79%

Big difference

Those who are most religious have learned that happiness is a state of mind (73%). On the other hand, those who are less religious have not really accepted this perspective so well (49%). This is a concern since religiosity is declining in Canada. *Where are people going to learn the personal values which are consistent with greater happiness?* If not through religion, we better start paying attention and learning from other sources.

Those who have their mind focused on money, and think about it most frequently are less happy. This is the wrong state-of-mind for happiness. The pursuit of money is not the right equation.

Frequency of Thinking about Money

	2+ times/wk	2-4 times/mo	Less often
Happy (scored 8 to 10)	29%	45%	57%

Another big difference

Those who do not appreciate that happiness is a state-of-mind are more likely to be thinking of money. It is as if happy people understand what happiness is about and focus on happiness as a state of mind (instead of happiness being a state of wealth). *Happy people value happiness in non-monetary terms.* And this is the easiest, most affordable, and quickest path to happiness; we just need to change our mentality!

THE HAPPINESS EQUATION

As we have reviewed, there are many separate elements which comprise happiness. I have summarized more than a dozen of the stronger influences, but there are also smaller elements. However, once we leave the general highlights to become more specific, we also get into smaller differences which may apply less and less in general and only to smaller subgroups of Canadians. This makes this review less useful since at the end we must recognize we are all like snowflakes. No two of us are the same.

We each have our own peculiarities, personalities, circumstantial issues, and unique genetic codes. Thus, it is safer to avoid prescribing too precise a set of characteristics for happiness, but rather to allow readers to interpret and adapt the general findings to apply the big ideas to themselves. Perhaps, in part, this complexity is why it is hard to define and understand happiness. It is simply not the easiest thing to peg down. But as said before, the good thing about happiness is we know when we are feeling it, and when we are not.

As a form of summary, one can review all of the many characteristics of happiness and make a formula, like a recipe for a cake. However, doing the modeling is tricky since many elements of happiness are interrelated. High personal debt may lead someone to work more hours each week to earn more money to pay down their debt load. In turn, they may have less time to exercise, and become less healthy. They may lose out on time to interact with friends, and they may be less charitable. All of these separate things also contribute to happiness. So, how do we summarize the formula or recipe for happiness?

Without getting too complicated, in the survey data which Ipsos collected for this book, I used a mathematical analysis which matched similar scoring characteristics of happiness into summary groups. This reduces the interrelationship which then allows me to more easily model the overall summary formula.

From the mathematical analysis of the survey, nine summary factors were found which form the recipe for happiness:

1. **Mental Peace-of-Mind:** current level of stress in life, current state of mental health, self-esteem and accomplishment of your goals.
2. **Financial Happiness:** level of wealth + income, current financial situation.
3. **Friends and Fun:** relationships with close friends, amount of time spend with friends, hobbies, interests, and pastimes.
4. **Physical Health:** satisfied with current state of health.
5. **Marital Status/Quality:** satisfied with marital/social status with regards to long-term relationship with partner.
6. **Family:** amount of time spend with family, relationships have with immediate family
7. **Job Quality:** satisfaction with employment situation.
8. **Charity:** amount of volunteering and financial support you contribute to your community.
9. **External Community:** current state of environmental issues, function of democracy in all levels of government.

Using these nine key generalized groups, the modeled formula for happiness creates the following recipe:

20% **Mental Peace-of-Mind/Stress**
+ 19% **Financial Happiness**
+ 18% **Friends/Fun**
+ 11% **Physical Health**
+ 11% **Marital Quality**
+ 8% **Family**
+ 8% **Job Quality**
+ 5% **Charity**
= *Happiness.*

(For the record, and for those keen-eyed readers who are wondering about the ninth factor from the previous page, the factor about "external community" with democracy, governments, and the environment, did not have a statistically significant role in describing the differences between happy Canadians versus unhappy Canadians. Perhaps this factor is more relevant in other nations where civility is less well delivered.)

More than any material thing, happiness is a state-of-mind. The key is to do what you are passionate about, and what excites you. This is about finding the right thing which jazzes you, and makes time fly by. It is getting into your zone. This may be a hobby, it may be your job, it may be helping others, it may be cooking, it may be running marathons, or whatever. The key is to find "it' because when you are in this zone, money matters less, stress drips off, and happiness increases the most.

Nonetheless, there is still a significant amount of happiness dependent on finances, income, and wealth. This begs the question: *"Does money buy happiness?"*

## CHAPTER 6

MONEY VERSUS HAPPINESS

"Money can't buy me love." – Paul McCartney

"A wise man should have money in his head, but not in his heart." – Jonathan Swift

DOES MONEY BUY HAPPINESS?

We discussed earlier how wealthier nations are happier nations. We also learned in our Canadian study that wealthier Canadians are happier than less wealthy Canadians. So, yes, wealth correlates with happiness...to a degree. Happiness was not so much tied to annual income levels, but rather was more strongly related to the differences in personal debt and net worth. In particular, those in debt are less happy. Whether it is individuals we are talking about, or nations, the *lack of wealth* creates *unhappiness,* but a lot of accumulated wealth does *not* necessarily create greater happiness.

The Ipsos survey tells us there are two distinct and almost opposing themes for happiness:

1) *Happiness is about values and a state of mind,* with a keen appreciation for a well-rounded and balanced life. It is about family and friends, relationships, community, charity, health, and sex. It is about doing what you are passionate about, with little regard for income. Money plays a small role in driving great happiness.

2) But *unhappiness occurs when one is in debt,* with a constant focus on money. This correlates with stress, a lack of control, and the feeling of being trapped. It also correlates with more time working, lower physical health,

less time doing hobbies, and less personal time.

To confirm this two-tiered approach to happiness, I reviewed the recipe of happiness (discussed in the previous chapter) by two groups: The characteristics of those who are happy (for those who scored 8, 9, or 10 on our 10-point life satisfaction scale), and separately the characteristics of those who are unhappy (those who scored just 1 to 6 on the 10- point scale). These characteristics are represented as two separate pie charts to show the recipe or proportion of the different characteristics for each group (next page). We do indeed see two different stories emerge from the mathematical modeling:

Those who are NOT happy are clearly more influenced by *money and stress*. Avoiding and minimizing debt is the most direct path for avoiding unhappiness.

On the other hand, the happiest people are affected by *non-monetary elements*. Without any debt, the path to happiness is *not* through greater accumulated wealth, but instead it is driven much more through self-esteem, doing what you are passionate about, and relationships with other people.

Perhaps it is worth repeating that we do not observe a difference in happiness by different annual income levels. It is financial debt which represents the key fiscal determinant of un-happiness rather than income.

Correlates of *Unhappiness*
(Share of influence among those who are unhappy)

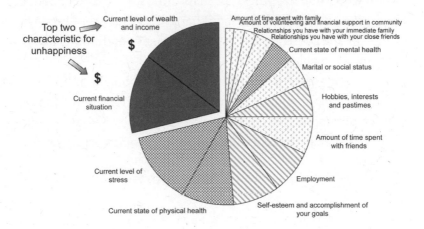

Correlates of *Happiness*
(Share of influence among those who are happy)

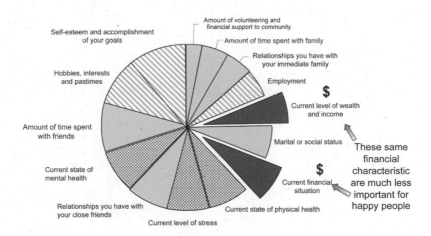

Who Is Thinking About What, and How Often?

Since happiness is largely a state-of-mind, especially for those who value happiness, perhaps it raises a curiosity about how often we are thinking about happiness and about money? What are the consequences or characteristics of thinking about money versus happiness?

How do you compare to the Canadian population? The two topics are about equal in consideration, with a slight edge in favour of happiness. Are you one of the keenest? About one in five Canadians are preoccupied with both topics on an almost daily basis.

<table>
<tr><th>How Often Think about Money?</th><th></th><th>How Often Think about Happiness?</th></tr>
<tr><td>10%</td><td>Don't really think about this</td><td>8%</td></tr>
<tr><td>7%</td><td>Less than once/month</td><td>8%</td></tr>
<tr><td>21%</td><td>1 to 3 times/month</td><td>16%</td></tr>
<tr><td>34%</td><td>About once a week</td><td>36%</td></tr>
<tr><td>29%</td><td>Daily, 2+ times/week</td><td>32%</td></tr>
</table>

Of the two characteristics, it is the frequent focus on *money* which appears to be more (negatively) impactful. Canadians who are constantly thinking of money seem to want more of it. On the other hand, Canadians who are constantly thinking of happiness are not really looking for more happiness. *The mentality of happiness is different than the mentality for money. The people thinking about happiness seem to value it "as it is."*

Think about Money:

	Near Daily	Weekly	Less/Don't
Happy (scored 8 to 10)	29%	45%	57%
Want more *Happiness*	33%	41%	57%
Want more *Money*	67%	59%	44%

People pre-occupied with money are less happy

Think about Happiness:

	Near Daily	Weekly	Less/Don't
Happy (scored 8 to 10)	41%	40%	44%
Want more *Happiness*	42%	41%	38%
Want more *Money*	58%	59%	62%

Where does this monetary preoccupation start? In addition to wanting material things, getting into debt is a main cause. Those with high levels of debt are much more likely to be thinking of money. Here is the profile of Canadians by their level of debt: High Levels, Some, and None.

Level of Financial Debt (all kinds combined)

	High	Some	None
Think about Money 2+ times a week	61%	40%	30%
Happy (scored 8 to 10)	23%	48%	53%
Satisfied with: Level of stress in life	11%	27%	38%
Level of self-esteem	31%	45%	52%
Relationships with family	54%	69%	69%
Relationships with friends	38%	56%	60%
Mental Health: Excellent or Very Good	47%	64%	69%
# Flues/Colds in the past 2 years	2.8	2.5	2.0
Age: 30 to 49 years old	56%	43%	24%
Have children under 18 years of age at home	47%	34%	21%

These are the benefits of not having debt

It is clear that this focus on money, with high debt, is coming at a physical, social, and family cost. Unfortunately, over one third of Canadians claim to have high levels of debt.

Getting Out and Staying Out of Debt

Owing to the significant impact debt has on driving *un*-happiness, and owing to the number of Canadians with high debt, it feels worthwhile to highlight some tips about debt management, and debt avoidance. I am not an expert, but talking about this with some financial planners, as well as simple research, common sense, and appreciating the benefits of staying out of debt, readers may wish to consider a few tips.

1) The first important element is to truly appreciate and internalize your motivation to reduce and stay out of debt. It is simply not worth it. Being in debt clearly leads to feelings of greater stress and less happiness. The cost of debt surpasses the gained experiences and material things acquired through the debt. Debt most

often outlives the short-term emotional highs which it affords. People in debt need to get motivated to get out of debt.

2) Paying interest on debt (and paying fees for bounced cheques) is equivalent of "paying for nothing."

    a. A single credit card, with a $1,000 debt, at 19% interest, will take about FIVE years to pay off if one is only making the minimum payment at $26 per month

    b. Pay more than the minimum monthly payments so you can pay down the principal as quickly as possible. To pay off the principal is the best investment you can likely ever make. You are paying with after-tax dollars, with a guaranteed "investment" rate equivalent to your interest rate. Paying interest "for nothing" is a guaranteed bad investment!

3) Avoid the trap of consumerism. If you do not need it, but want it, stop to realize that your emotions are about to get you into trouble. Humans are not rational, and we often are driven by emotional desires. Realize that marketing, retail, and consumerism is in the business of creating *desire*. It is natural to be tempted. But it is also smart to recognize it and say "no." Frankly, it is empowering to say no, knowing at the end of the day you are better off for avoiding debt.

4) Help yourself avoid impulsive emotional purchasing:

    a. Monitor your monthly expenses to find your pattern. Make a budget for what you can afford to spend on frivolous "wants" versus the things you need to buy.

    b. Have a cash buffer. Save up to afford the bigger "wants."

   c. Open a second bank account; one for living expenses which you need to pay each month, and the second as a "savings" account for more discretionary funds. You may also wish to consider a third account as a long-term savings or "emergency" fund. This can be the buffer for unexpected purchases which need to be made.

   d. Identify your weaknesses! Which expense categories are likely to get you into trouble? Avoid those stores! Stay out of the malls if you cannot control your impulses to shop. Replace this with other activities you are passionate about.

   e. Pay with cash. You can only spend what you already have. There are no interest fees paying with cash! Leave the credit and debit cards at home.

   f. Plan ahead before you leave home or before you take money out of the bank machine. Decide in advance what you can afford or want to afford.

   g. Shop with a friend, and tell them to talk you out of buying certain items. Tell them in advance that you do not want to spend more than X dollars. Have them be your second conscience. Hopefully, they will be less emotionally engaged.

   h. Agree to discuss any potential purchase over a certain amount (for example, $50) with your spouse, partner, or friend. ("Am I crazy to buy this today?")

5) If you are going to get a loan or a mortgage, live within your means. Purchasing a house or car is often emotional. Do not get attracted to buy more than you can really afford. Ask the banker, a friend, and others for advice. Recognize that your emotions may again get you into trouble.

   a. If the budget item is significant, get three quotes.

   b. Consider waiting at least 2-3 weeks since many emotional impulses will pass by then.

   c. The bigger the down-payment against the purchased item, the better.

   d. Lock in the mortgage or loan rate at the level you can afford. Avoid rising payments which you cannot afford. This plan is often better than the risk of staying flexible in hope of paying less interest. If you cannot afford the fixed, locked-in rates now, then chances are you are over-extending your debt load.

6) If you have more than one source of debt, with interest payments, make a list and rank them in the order of the interest rate. It is not the size of the debt or the size of the required monthly payments which matter. The problem is the price or cost of the debt based on the interest rate you pay. It may feel good to pay off a lower amount of debt to close it, but if the interest rate is higher on some other debt, then focus on the highest rate. Interest is interest regardless of the size of the debt it is based upon.

   a. Stop allowing your debt to increase. Get involved and feel like you are helping to manage the debt payments rather than ignoring the bad news and having things spiral out of control. It will be empowering to take some control, even if you are stuck with the problem for a long while.

   b. Realize that it takes time to get out of debt (likely, just like it took time to get into such a problem). The day you start to do something to manage your debt problems, then the sooner you will get better control and feel empowered about taking charge.

   c. Consider consolidating the debt. There are serv-

ices to help combine and renegotiate the higher interest levels into more manageable and reasonable
payments.

d. Negotiate with those whom you have debt. It is in
their interest to get paid. Getting something from
you is better than nothing, so work with them.
Simply hearing from you is helpful. This alone can
prevent them from coming after you with collec-
tion agencies. Even banks will renegotiate if they
see you have a very high debt load and are at risk
of defaulting. Work with them. They need you to
succeed as well.

e. If you get automatic salary payment at work, or
payments from other sources into a bank account,
ask for it to be split into two accounts, one for
monthly expenses, and the other to help pay down
the debt.

f. Can you re-mortgage your house to help consoli-
date other (high interest) debt, into one more
easily managed debt program? (Be cautious that
you do not put the ownership of your house at
risk!)

7) There are non-profit (charitable) services for managing
debt. Consider soliciting their help. Leave your pride
aside as best possible, and ask for help. Your pride can
be repaired, and is likely more affordable than your interest costs ("paying for nothing").

Doing What You Are Passionate About!

On a cheerier note, focusing on and doing the things
which we are passionate about is great for our quality of life.
As we observed earlier, those who spend the most time doing
what they are excited or passionate about are much happier.

And this happiness is often much more affordable than what debt will buy you.

In the Canadian study, we can observe that people doing what they are passionate about are not earning higher income, are not working more, are not sleeping more, are not more (or less) religious. Instead, this happiness comes from determining what you are good at doing; what you enjoy doing; and then arranging your life (as best possible) to be able to do more of it. This can be a hobby, a pastime, volunteering, or even meaningful work. If there is something at work you like doing, ask to be able to do more of it (which is likely going to be more rewarding than simply earning a higher income doing something which you are not so excited about). Below, we can see the real significant benefits associated to the people who are doing what they are most passionate about...

Hours/Week on Activities for Which You Are Passionate

	0 to 6 hours	7 to 13 hours	14 + hours
Happy (scored 8 to 10)	35%	42%	61%
Aware of strengths + weaknesses	56%	59%	71%
Feel in control of my life	32%	32%	44%
Satisfied with self-esteem	36%	43%	52%
Satisfied with level of stress in life	22%	24%	33%
Average # hours work/week	26.4	20.2	22.5
Average # hours sleep/night	6.9	6.9	7.0
Income: Less than $50,000	39%	45%	37%
More than $75,000	35%	30%	37%
Have a *meaningful* job	30%	26%	42%
Opportunity to do what good at doing	31%	32%	49%

Few differences here | Noticeable characteristics for those do what they are passionate about.

CHAPTER 7

WHAT TO EXPECT.
LOOKING FORWARD.

"The best way to predict the future is to create it." — Peter Drucker

HAPPINESS THROUGH OUR AGES

It feels a little strange talking about happiness by different age groups since there is very little we can do about this. The only solution is to live longer! Regardless, I find it curious that the least happy point in our lives appears to be in the child-bearing years, when more Canadians have young children at home. It feels like we have been brought up to believe having children is a happy and rewarding experience. Whether we wish to admit it or not, there is a direct correlation between having children and being less happy. With children come sacrifices, stress, financial debt, loss of "me time," and so on. On the other hand, as the children grow older and more independent, happiness among parents increases. The following chart maps out the happiness by age of Canadians.

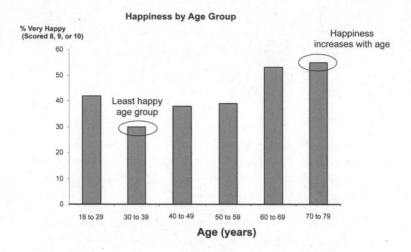

Happiness by Age Group

% Very Happy
(Scored 8, 9, or 10)

Happiness increases with age

Least happy age group

Age (years)

18 to 29   30 to 39   40 to 49   50 to 59   60 to 69   70 to 79

Source: Ipsos Survey of Canadian Adults, June 2010

Greater happiness among older Canadians may also be due to greater wisdom among the older generations. Perhaps older adults have learned over time that money does not buy happiness. They accept being themselves, "as they are," instead of trying to be someone else, or trying to achieve something unattainable. It begs the question: If younger adults can learn this concept at an earlier age can they be happier sooner?

There are also other interesting correlations with older age and key factors of happiness such as: greater religiosity, less debt, more accumulated wealth, more volunteerism, greater charity, and so on. However, when I teased out the different relationships (for example, older age versus greater religiosity, and older age versus better financial status), it is clear that older age by itself has a large influence on happiness (regardless of the other inter-relating elements). *Simply growing old is a good strategy for greater happiness!*

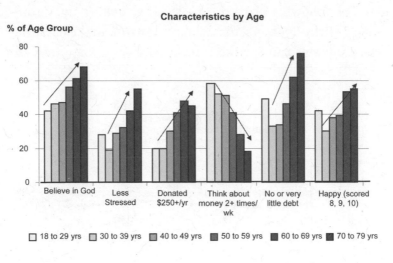

Characteristics by Age

% of Age Group

☐ 18 to 29 yrs ☐ 30 to 39 yrs ☐ 40 to 49 yrs ■ 50 to 59 yrs ■ 60 to 69 yrs ■ 70 to 79 yrs

Source: Ipsos Survey of Canadian Adults, June 2010

If we look at the size of the age groups within Canada, as a whole nation, we can observe that there are a disproportionate number of adults born in the years 1947 to 1966, and a lesser number born 1967 to 1979. These are the "Baby Boomers," and "Baby Bust," respectively, which readers are most likely aware. With an uneven distribution of population by decade we can recognize that the nature of our total population will change as the different age groups (cohorts) grow older. As the Baby Boomers age, and since there are so many of them, this age cohort will affect how Canada feels as a whole...

So, what might we expect for Canada over the next 40 years? If we project all the different age cohorts forward in time to 2050, we can reasonably hope to see a *constant level of happiness in Canada overall (all other things being constant)*. That is, as the Boomers age, we can expect to see a slight increase in happiness in the older people, but this is offset a little by the Baby Echo who will be less happy.

The following chart tracks each age cohort (age groups such as Baby Boomers, the Echo, and so on). In the dark thick black line, we can see the forecasted level of happiness for Canada as a whole...

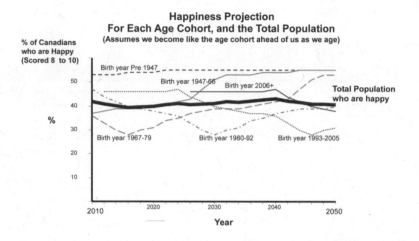

(Forecasting is provided courtesy of the Seefeld Group Cohort Model. Seefeld Group (www.seefeldgroup.com) is a Montréal-based integrated marketing agency specializing in developing and implementing actionable marketing strategies. Their cohort model is a market analysis and forecasting tool which provides insight into past and future differences in attitudes and consumption levels among generational groups. Combining survey results with Canadian census data, behaviours are projected by birth year groupings (also known as "cohorts"), and then applied to tailored population projections yielding medium to long term forecasts. The results are customized quantitative insight on the impact of evolving Canadian demographic trends on industries or public policy topics, such as an aging society.)

However, when making forecasts based on age cohorts and demographics, there is an important consideration about what assumptions to make. In the above forecast *I assumed* that younger Canadians pay off their debt, learn the wisdom of current older Canadians, and become similarly happy like older Canadians. That is, the above forecast assumes younger adults will become exactly like the older adults when they achieve the respective age. But perhaps this is not the best assumption! Perhaps, instead, we should be assuming that young adults

will be more overweight than the age cohort ahead, be less religious, have higher personal debt loads, and donate less!? This
is a more accurate reflection of the recent historic trends in
Canada, and these trends are not so likely to suddenly change.

For Religiosity: It is likely best to assume that as the Canadian population evolves forward we will not gain in religiosity,
but will continue to trend towards greater atheism. This has
been the overall trend for the past 50 years.

Personal Debt: Debt also has a big influence on happiness
and differs by age group. If younger adults carry a greater portion of their personal debt forward into older age we may very
well have a crankier Canadian population. Since we have been
experiencing an increasing personal debt load in Canada for
the past 25 years, it is likely safe to assume that Canadians will
not be paying off as much debt as we currently observe among
older Canadians (born during the Depression and World War
II).

Health: Currently, the young adults 18 to 29 years exercise
more often, and are less likely to be overweight. If this group
can maintain their same current levels of exercise and body
weight as they age, we would have a significantly healthier and
happier society. However, obesity rates have been increasing
in Canada, so it is not so realistic to expect obesity rates to remain like they are today across the age cohorts. If we assume
higher obesity rates we can expect a less healthy population as
the different age cohorts grow older.

Charity: How altruism plays out is a little hard to forecast.
On one hand, young Canadians seem to be more aware and involved in charitable causes, but it is the older Canadians who
actually give more, and volunteer more. And with an increasing personal debt crisis in Canada (among the young), there
may be less discretionary money to donate to charitable causes.
Thus, our license to assume that altruism will increase with

age is questionable at this point.

The following chart summarizes these four characteristics discussed above, forecast forward using the Seefeld Group population cohort simulation. This weights the size of each age cohort by their proportions, over the next 40 years. Instead of assuming we will each become like the age group ahead of us as we grow older, I adjusted the characteristics as follows, to reflect the above based on our recent trends. You can judge if I have been too extreme:

- For our financial debts, I assumed the situation for the next 10 years would see Canadians with 10% more debt (than the age cohort ahead of them), 20% more debt for the following 15 years, and 30% more the next 15 years to the year 2050.

- For health, for the next 10 years, I assumed we become more overweight by 10% higher levels (versus the age cohort ahead), 15% more overweight for the following 15 years, and 20% more overweight for the next 15 years until the year 2050.

- For charity, I assumed the rate of donations to be 10% less (of current rates found among the age cohort ahead) for the next 10 years, 15% less for the following 15 years, and 20% less for the next 15 years until the year 2050.

- For religiosity, I assumed no changes. That is, our levels remain with us, unchanged, as we grow older. We do not become more religious (like the age cohort ahead as currently exists today).

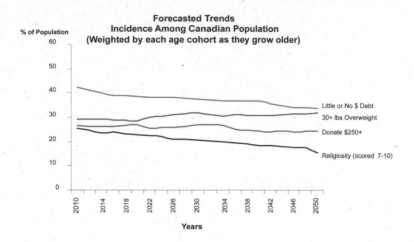

These above trends are some of the very factors which comprise happiness. They are trending down, and may very well lead to a decline in happiness in Canada. (The above implies about a five point drop in happiness from 42% to 37%, for Canadians scoring 8 to 10 on the 10-point scale, and a corresponding increase in unhappiness).

Do you get the sense by now that we need to do something different? If we continue to increase our rates of obesity, with greater debt loads, less religiosity, lower participation in charity, all in pursuit of money and material things, we are going to drive our nation into the ground. We are going to become ever more stressed, crankier, less civil, and with a shorter life expectancy.

CHAPTER 8

PERHAPS WE NEED A
NEW NON-RELIGION

*"We can live without religion and meditation, but we
cannot survive without human affection."*
— Tenzin Gyatso, 14th Dalai Lama

WHO HAS THE RESPONSIBILITY FOR OUR HAPPINESS?

In the previous chapter, we observed that our future forecast for happiness is not so positive. Many of the factors which
support happiness are declining.

With the social trend towards less religion in our lives, it
appears we have a real need to find a substitute for the lost
benefits of religion (for those who are not religious in behaviour). We need something which offers the same benefits of
religion, but without necessarily requiring Canadians to be
more religious. We need an initiative to get Canadians to be
more community oriented, more connected, more charitable,
and less mercenary. This will lead to a happier and more civil
Canada.

To have a happier and more civil society, it appears worthwhile for our governments to (1) make it harder for Canadians
to get into debt (especially unmanageable levels of debt), and
(2) to help Canadians manage and pay off their debt loads.

We need Canada's current ParticipACTION program to
promote greater exercise. This seems to be a most appropriate government initiative. Good health correlates with greater
happiness.

Similar to the ParticipACTION program to promote

greater exercise in Canada, we need a national program to promote national altruism. Helping others is a national public
"good." This will protect civility, and provide for more happy
Canadians.

A fond definition for insanity is doing the same thing over
and over again but expecting a different outcome.

We need to change our approach to life to get back on to
our natural evolutionary trajectory. This will require a collective
effort. But fortunately, it works at the individual level as well,
one by one. We can improve our own life. And if we wish to
help our tribe, we can also work collectively towards a better
Canada.

In fact, it is not just me feeling this way. Many (but not all)
Canadians feel a need to take a greater responsibility for ourselves. In our Ipsos survey we asked Canadians about responsibilities. Here are the questions, and I have inserted the mean
average score from the results of the survey. On which side of
the average do you fall?

Q.10 For each of the next questions there is a range between opposing views. How would you place yourself between the opposing views? Please score anywhere from 1 to 10 for each question. The more strongly you feel, score more towards 1 or towards 10. The triangles below indicate how Canadians scored in the survey

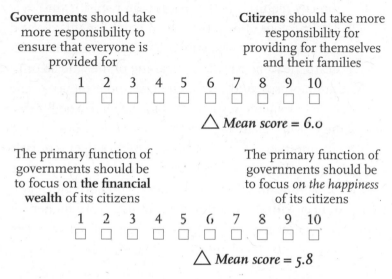

| **Governments** should take more responsibility to ensure that everyone is provided for | | | | | | | | | **Citizens** should take more responsibility for providing for themselves and their families |

1 2 3 4 5 6 7 8 9 10

△ *Mean score* = 6.0

| The primary function of governments should be to focus on **the financial wealth** of its citizens | | | | | | | | | The primary function of governments should be to focus *on the happiness* of its citizens |

1 2 3 4 5 6 7 8 9 10

△ *Mean score* = 5.8

Clearly I am not alone in thinking that everyday citizens need to step up and do something to help. It would be nice for our governments to focus more on things which increase happiness rather than just financial wealth. Both of these points of view are in the majority in Canada.

ARE THE BENEFITS OF RELIGION DUE TO GOD?

Earlier in this book we found many beneficial correlations associated with religiosity. The thing about correlations is that they do not prove cause and effect. And this is important when reviewing the benefits of religion because *it may very well be that many of the benefits we observe are not directly due to belief in a god.* Many benefits of organized religion may be due to the sense of community, stepping away from our busy lives, en-joying a beautiful building (with singing and nice music), participating in organized events, helping others, seeing friends, and so on. That is, perhaps there are two types of ben-efits of religion for humanity:

(1) The *social and community* benefits (which do not directly require a belief in a superior spirit), and

(2) The theological benefits: The mental benefits derived from specifically believing in a god (including life after death, heaven, salvation, meaning of life, and so on).

Within the Ipsos study, we do indeed find evidence of the *social benefits* of religion (regardless of the belief in a god). If we look at the 51% of Canadians who *absolutely believe in God*, and split them into two groups based on whether they regularly participate in religious services, versus those who do not, we find some significant differences. Those who have the oppor-tunity to meet with their congregations also score higher for many of the social and civil benefits of religion. The benefits of religion are not just theological.

BELIEVERS: ATTEND RELIGIOUS SERVICES VS DO NOT ATTEND

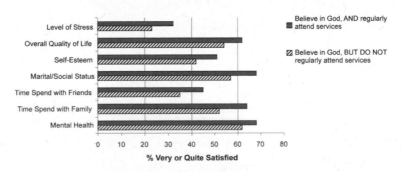

Source: Ipsos Survey of Canadian Adults, June 2010

The above chart suggests that the *social aspects* of being religious offer many benefits which do not come simply from believing in a god. Perhaps many of the benefits of religion are strongly attached to the *human nature* of our evolution; namely, to be connected and to be an active participant in the community (the tribe). This matches the concept from evolutionists which suggests that religion helps unite the tribe (which enhances better survival). The above chart supports this idea of community, as does the following chart. Here, we see religious people feel more connected and accepted than those who are less religious. Practising Canadians feel a greater sense of belonging in their community versus non-practising Canadians...

"I Feel I Have a Good Sense of Belonging and Acceptance in My Community"

Source: Ipsos Survey of Canadian Adults, June 2010

WHAT IF NON-RELIGIOUS PEOPLE AND SOCIETY IN GENERAL, DID MORE OF WHAT RELIGIOUS PEOPLE DO?

What if we interacted better within our communities; visited beautiful buildings to relax and appreciated live organ music; participated in a singing program; were friendlier with others; helped those in need; organized group events (such as garage sales, fund-raisers, family picnics); and listened to nice stories about people doing good deeds? Might this make us happier? The evidence indicates "yes"!

I appreciate that the belief in a god offers additional (theological) benefits for humans. The Ipsos study shows this. However, can all humans, and especially for the growing sector who are not so religious, learn from those who are more religious to experience the *non-theological* benefits for greater civility? Can we become happier by mimicking some of the social, friendly, and charitable practices of the religious, without necessarily believing in a god?

Said another way, as our Canadian society becomes less religious, we would likely find appealing benefits by having similar social and community-oriented activities which promote civility, friendship, kindness, charity, and understanding. Our happiness is based on these characteristics.

CHAPTER 9

GETTING ON WITH BEING HAPPIER

"Happiness doesn't depend upon who you are or what you have; it depends solely on what you think." – Dale Carnegie

THE EVOLUTIONARY EQUATION OF TRUE HAPPINESS

So what have we learned? The key to happiness correlates with our evolutionary past, and not with accumulated wealth. Happiness is about our health, our passion, our ability to love, the warmth of helping others, our response to stress, and so much more. These are the things that make us human. Happiness does not come from materialistic things. For 99.9% of our evolution, we did not have such materialism, nor great accumulated wealth. In turn, if we recognize and appreciate a few things, we can become more like the happiest Canadians. It starts (and ends) in our minds. Your happiness is within your control, and you can start working on it today. Here is what we have covered about the evolutionary nature of happiness...

1) Happiness comes from within the mind.

   a. One of the life's secrets is to learn that *living is a struggle* for each and everyone one of us. Life is tough. We are genetically programmed to always have some unhappiness to avoid complacency. Even when things are going well, we grow accustomed to it, de-sensitize, and re-calibrate to allow unhappiness to seep back in. This is clearly evident. We have seen a three-fold increase in wealth in North America since World War II, and an incredible increase in our standards of living, and yet we are not happier! We need to appreciate that life is a constant struggle, and that *periods of unhappiness are normal.*

b. Happiness is largely a state of mind. Happiness is all about how we approach it, define it, judge it, and think about it. The simplest, most affordable, and fastest path to greater happiness is for us to *lower our expectations* and change how we think about happiness.

c. Do not let other people define *your* happiness. Determine how you feel in absolute. *Comparing to others is an ill-advised approach* for judging happiness. It wrongly appears that others are having more fun, more often. Like the trees in the forest, we will never win by competing. We are smarter than the trees, and should judge our happiness in absolute, in our own minds.

d. *Appreciate what you have.* Realize that always wanting more is not the path to lasting happiness. Wanting is based on dopamine in the brain, whereas on-going happiness is tied to serotonin throughout the body. As my grandfather frequently said: "Happiness is wanting what you have rather than having what you want." Good advice.

e. Appreciate that *humans make poor short-term decisions based largely on emotional judgments.* The closer the expected pay-off of a decision, the more we are biased by our emotions and desires. We often know better, but frequently give into our emotional "wants." This is why diets, saving money, and exercising are so hard. We know what is best, but we struggle with the emotional desire, in the moment, to do what is best. The more we can learn to resist short-term emotional "wants," the better we will feel after. Our darn short-term emotional desires often lead to our long-term regrets!

    f. Be more critical about what money buys, and more aware of the personal sacrifice or "cost" to earn more. Do not use money as the decision-criterion for your happiness.

2) *Avoid debt* with a strong determination. If you are in debt, work hard to get out of it. Debt is the biggest driver of unhappiness, and comes with stress and many other side effects. The stress related to debt literally reduces our health. Avoid short-term temptations which might cost money leading to greater credit card or personal debt. The debt will cause more unhappiness than giving into the short-term desire of the purchase. This can't be stressed enough.

3) *Do what you are passionate about.* This is one of the biggest drivers of happiness among happy Canadians. The happiest people know what they are good at doing, and what excites them. They then spend more time doing it. Orient and negotiate your life to spend more time doing what you are passionate about at work, as a hobby, through a non-profit group, outdoors in nature, or whatever excites you. Involving yourself in what you are passionate about has more impact on feeling happy than earning more money or buying things.

4) *Reduce screen time, get out, and connect with others.* Make an effort to interact with others more often. We have evolved as social beings and need to recognize the soft intangible benefits of being with friends and interesting people. Laugh, share stories, and discuss problems.

5) *Aim to be physically active and as healthy as you can be.*
   This is not about vanity and a beauty contest. This is
   simply about your own health and well-being.

6) If you are not so religious, *act like religious people* (without having to necessarily be religious). Appreciate
   civility, peace, understanding, and acceptance of others.
   Support others, and be an active member in your community. Take a few hours off for personal time to reflect
   on your self, your family, and on being a good person.
   Ask yourself how you can be a better person.

7) *Help others who need a hand. Volunteer, and make donations.* Aim to live with 97% of your income and to share
   3% with the needy, and volunteer a few hours a month.
   This adds meaning to our lives and induces a sense of
   empowerment. It is fulfilling to know you are part of
   the solution to some of the social problems we face
   (rather than being part of the problem). Apathy is not
   very rewarding, and is often accompanied with guilt.
   The best way to realize the warm feelings is to find a
   cause in your town which interests you. Learn more
   about the charity or non-profit organization, meet some
   of those involved, personalize the relationship, and get
   involved. Make it about people. Make it personal. This
   is much more rewarding than sending money to insti-
   tutionalized charities, staffed with strangers, without
   any real sense that you are indeed making a difference.

8) *Make a plan to be happy.* Consider the above, and what
   you can do to help improve your future. In the words of
   John F. Kennedy: *Let us not seek to fix the blame for the
   past. Let us accept our own responsibility for the future.*

And so we have come to a simple overall summary, which
is as old is our species: The secret to our happiness is found in
our natural evolution. It is a perspective about what truly

matters. It is not an expensive pursuit. Fortunately, our evolutionary ancestors did not have the opportunity to get into financial debt.

For those with a little extra interest in charity, helping others, and altruism, I share with you a little more about our evolutionary characteristics, and the type of society which appears to be the happiest. This takes us a little beyond our individual happiness equation. This shares a point of view about altruism, and a civil society...

ASIDE:

CHARITABLE GIVING IN CANADA

"It is every man's obligation to put back into the world at least the equivalent of what he takes out of it." – Albert Einstein

Our happiness equation comprises many different elements. Being charitable is just one aspect. However, unlike many other characteristics, charity has a huge multiplier benefit since it enriches both the lives of donors and the lives of the many recipients. This chapter represents the real opportunity to leverage this multiplier effect to make for a much happier, kinder, compassionate, and civil Canada.

A BIRTHDAY CARD FROM GRANNY

My maternal grandparents were personable, extremely caring, very philanthropic, and strongly family oriented. All of these characteristics came together in a special club they created for their 24 grandchildren. They called it "Club 21."

When each of us turned 21 years old, a letter arrived from our maternal grandparents, with a cheque for $500. "Happy Birthday," it read. "Here is $500... but it is not for you!" The letter went on to say that the money was to be given to five separate charities. The letter explained the rules, reminding us of less fortunate people in the world and pointing out our charitable responsibility as part of the next generation. Granny informed us that it was our obligation to help those along the road of life who needed our help. There will always be people in need.

We were each instructed to choose five charities and to give each $100. Two of the charities had to be in the province we were residing, two in the province of Quebec where we grew up, and one from anywhere else. We then had to write to our grandparents explaining which charities we chose and why. Once we completed this last task, we were welcomed into "Club 21" and we received another $500 cheque to spend on ourselves.

I am the 21st grandchild so I knew what to expect from my older siblings. I did my task very quickly! This was our birthday present, with strings attached. And this was just one of the ways our grandparents worked to teach us our social responsibility to help those less well off.

Teaching and encouraging philanthropy, be it five dollars or $5,000, is something we need to do. Giving and volunteering is a learned behaviour. Those who are taught to give and who have family members who contribute to charity become more caring and giving early on and throughout their lives.

Do you have young children, nieces, nephews or grandchildren you might start on the road to giving? It could be "Club 21" or you could do it differently. But one thing is clear. The future needs you to get them started today, and there is lot of room for more members in Club 21. Is there someone you can teach or encourage?

Is Altruism Natural?

The concept of altruism seems to contradict the rules of evolution. The idea of giving away and weakening one's own situation is not so natural. This challenges the importance of looking after our self above all else. It begs the question: Does altruism really exist?

Some psychologists and evolutionists would suggest that altruism is all part of game theory. By giving to the tribe to help others, the donor benefits through greater acceptance in the tribe. The donor may also gain good favour, more influence, and a greater say in control of the tribe. By giving to others in the tribe, we are indebting others to help us when we might need help in the future. By being altruistic, we are in fact gaining and strengthening our own position. In turn, helping others is not truly altruistic because the costs of giving are reciprocated by the benefits. It might look like altruism, but the benefits are real, and match the costs.

We may also gain in more internal (emotional), and less obvious ways from altruism. Owing to our strong mental capacities, perhaps the gains of altruism are largely felt internally as a warm feeling, a sense of satisfaction, self-esteem, and fulfillment of duty (whether imposed by culture, social norms, religion, or upbringing). Perhaps conforming to the norms and pressures of the community provide the motivating feelings to justify doing so. This might be out of guilt, and/or it might truly provide the donor with a warm and lasting feeling of "doing good."

In the charity sector, one may argue that many donors do not actually give up much when they donate money. Wealthier people simply give more because they can afford to, and not because they are specifically more altruistic. They are not likely suffering greater amounts of "cost" for their larger philanthropy. The amount given often does not affect the donor's standard of living, their health, or their survival fitness. Frankly, you might argue that public philanthropy also offers direct social benefits through an elevated status of having made a (significant) donation. For those who volunteer their time, the same applies. Perhaps the benefits of volunteering one's time is actually very rewarding to the volunteer such that their behaviour is not so altruistic in the pure sense. Again, the benefit might equal or even surpass the "cost." We also can't forget that in many developed nations, we get a charitable tax receipt in return for donating.

ALTRUISTIC BEHAVIOUR IS WHAT MATTERS

Since we cannot really measure the internal psychology and emotional feelings associated with philanthropy and volunteerism, it is very difficult to prove or deny if the "costs" exceed the (emotional) "benefits." *Perhaps it is this distinction between altruistic motivation versus altruistic behaviour that matters most in this discussion.*

If we focus on altruistic *behaviour*, do we find situations which appear to have more cost to the donor than the benefit?

Clearly, the answer is yes. In moments of crisis from natural disaster, people thousands of miles away are making donations to disaster relief efforts. They are giving to strangers. The recipients will never know or have the opportunity to return the favour. There is no reasonable expectation of a mutually returned gain for the donor. It is hard to see that this is a pre-determined self-serving behaviour. We have also heard stories of heroes stepping in to help others in danger (danger of drowning, of being trapped in a burning building, in hiding Jews from the Nazis, and so on). These acts of altruism are done almost without rational thinking, and at great risk. The gain is not worth the cost in many cases, since the "cost" is the donor's own life. When interviewed, these heroes often fail to explain their motivation. They simply saw someone in danger and acted. This implies a sense of empathy and compassion beyond the self-serving nature of self preservation.

Altruistic behaviour is also found in many other different species, especially those which are social and live in groups. For example, Vervet monkeys give alarm calls to warn fellow monkeys of the presence of predators even though their actions may attract greater attention to themselves, increasing their personal chance of being attacked. Dolphins support sick or injured animals, swimming under them for hours at a time and pushing them to the surface so they can breathe. Wolves bring meat back to members of the pack not present at the kill. Walruses have been seen adopting orphans who lost their parents to predators. Bees and wasps devote their whole lives to the maximum benefit of their hive. They spend their life caring for the queen, building and defending the hive, bringing food, and parenting the queen's larvae.

A Genetic Explanation for Altruism

The justification for such altruistic behaviour in the animal kingdom rests in the fact that the survival and well being of the tribe is also beneficial to our genetic evolution (above and beyond the importance of any one member). That is, there are benefits to having a strong, happy, balanced tribe, which in turn has rewarded this altruistic characteristic in so many species. That is, we have gained this altruistic feeling through genes which are actually helping the tribe more than helping the individual organism. A healthier tribe leads to healthier tribal members, which in turn benefits the reproduction of the very genes which drive altruism (regardless of what happens to any one tribe member).

A Natural Tendency Toward Equality

Through our evolutionary development of compassion and altruism, we have not simply abandoned our self-interests! Altruism is not rampant across Canada, and we do not live in equality. We are still largely driven by selfish voices in our heads asking: "What's in it for me? Why should I care?"

In conjunction with our selfish nature, through our evolution, we have *also* developed a tendency to equality. In our ancestral tribes, if any one person became too powerful or influential, it represented a threat to others. There has been a constant pressure between any one individual trying to be powerful, versus the interest of the tribe trying to prevent too much power. It is not so useful to be manipulated, bullied, taken advantage of, or over-powered by others. If any one tribe member became too powerful, it was in the interest of everyone else to bring the person down. Equality was a much more advantageous way to survive in a tribe. This has been the evolutionary nature which comprises our species today. Through our history, many dictatorships have fallen, and those which exist do not thrive well. Communities work better through freedom of the individual, and in a balanced democracy.

LARGE URBAN POPULATIONS DISTORT
THE MECHANISMS OF OUR TRIBAL WAYS

With the invention of currency in our modern world, and with free capitalistic economies, it is much easier for people to accumulate great wealth. And with the creation of huge cities, the concept of tribal equality and the ability to restore balance seems to have been lost. Our tribes are now so large that we can no longer influence the tribal members as we have in the past.

Regardless, we need to remind ourselves that no one gets wealthy by themselves. To accumulate wealth requires a society of buyers, a network of workers, and a social structure to facilitate it. We need to remind the more successful tribe members of the greater needs of the tribe. There is an obligation to share some of the wealth with the very society that contributes to it. If a successful tribe member does not reciprocate and support the tribe, we should collectively work to kick the tribe member out of our tribe (to bring them down).

Furthermore, the obligation is to the current generation and not to future generations which have done nothing to contribute to this good fortune. In a sense, it is immoral to take from one generation, and give it to a future generation (though inheritance, and charitable foundations).

There is also the recognition that many of today's institutions, from which we have individually and personally benefited, were created by others. Many schools, libraries, community centres, hospitals, parks, museums, charitable services, and so on, have been made possible by generous charitable support from previous donors and volunteers. For those who have benefited, there is a certain obligation to pay back what has already been consumed, and/or will likely be further enjoyed.

The challenge is to appreciate that our tribe has become too big and full of strangers to work so well in obliging the necessary support. We have lost the ancestral ability to demand equality and balance within the tribe. Indeed, in many developed nations, the rich are getting richer. In the pure capitalist society, the community cannot so easily suppress the dominant wealthy power brokers. Money buys power. The electorate needs to understand that their society needs some legal mechanisms (namely taxation) to force greater equality and balance. Interestingly, many of the happiest nations in the world are also quite socialistic, with higher top tax brackets than those found in the United States. Higher taxes and social programs share the wealth and benefit the collective tribe, leading to a more civil and happy society. This is not about preaching communism, but it does suggest that civility and social support is a preferred path to greater happiness (more so than pure capitalism and freedom of unrestricted greed). Until we self-correct our social trends, there needs to be community pressure and a moral obligation to be charitable, to be more civil, and with greater compassion.

THE PATH TO A GOOD CIVIL SOCIETY

What kind of society is best for our species? What makes

for the greatest happiness? For most of our evolution, the ancestral tribes were a manageable size. However, in more recent times, our population has exploded in numbers, with a strong movement to urbanization. The majority of the population now lives in cities and towns where we have become neighbourhoods of strangers. The old tribal systems of civil interaction and civil behaviour no longer work the same way.

Michael Edwards, in his book *Civil Society* spells out a convincing path for a good civil society. Edwards argues that "civil association" (people power) is the preferred model for society (versus a pure profit incentive economy and versus a state-run society). However, since many civil associations will act in their own self-interest to the detriment of the public (as one extreme example, consider the Ku Klux Klan), we need checks and balances. This is where the role of government comes in.

We need to have freedom of association to create community initiatives to address our communities' interests, but with a certain level of rules and restrictions to prevent some associations acting in a dysfunctional manner against the collective interests of the greater good. Pure freedom and democracy allow for greed to run amok since our tribes have become too big to manage such an imbalance. Greed and the pursuit of wealth, power, and influence have proven to be not so good to the greater interests of the whole society. The sociological trends in America since World War II are indicative of what happens in one of the freest and wealthiest democracies which values freedom over civility. It does not lead to greater happiness, nor one of the happiest cultures.

Without going too much further down this philosophical and practical debate about what types of society, government, laws, rights, religions, and so on is best (for which there will never be a consensus), it appears that no one extreme view is likely best. To accommodate the vast range of views, some form of compromise is necessary. We will likely do best with some form of society that is in the middle between communism and free democracy + capitalism. Government policy, tax incentives, and even direct government funding are needed to support "public good" initiatives and to encourage the desired social association (and restriction of dysfunctional associations). We need a role for government to facilitate philanthropy to support those in our communities that need help.

A CIVIL SOCIETY IS *VERY CANADIAN*

Unlike Americans, who largely oppose government involvement in society, Canadians are more accepting of the already major role government plays in our lives. Perhaps some Canadians are so accepting of government in our lives that these individuals have abandoned their own sense of responsibilities in society. They have suspended their obligations, responsibilities, and moral motivations to play a constructive role. Frankly, some of the more socialistic countries in the developed world also have comparatively low rates of philanthropy (as a percentage of GDP). This is our challenge in Canada when we compare our lower levels of philanthropy versus our American neighbours.

Thus, as much as we need a certain role of government in our civil society, we must not also simply suspend our own individual responsibility to help those in need. There is no doubt that there is still unmet need in Canadian society (the sick, homeless, battered, mentally ill, disadvantaged, and so on). We each have an obligation as a member of the tribe to be compassionate and supportive. This has been our evolutionary way, and it leads to a happier and more civil society. It is also rewarding and meaningful to the individual.

A CARING NATION HELPS OTHERS IN NEED!

Canada is a caring nation. Our global reputation is one of peace, civility, and acceptance of others. So why are we so poor in donating to charity and volunteering our time in Canada? We are losing out on an opportunity to feel fulfilled, helpful, and happy.

Canadians, on average, donate half as much per person as Americans, despite the average Canadian being wealthier. Although 87% of Canadians give annually to charities, we give very little. The median donation level is just $120 annually. Overall, the average level of donation in Canada is less than 0.8% of income, and for those with higher income ($100,000 or more), the percentage drops even lower to half of 1% (0.5%).

The Canada Revenue Agency reports that in 2007, prior to the start of the recession, only 24% of tax returns claimed a charitable tax receipt. This is a 4% drop from the previous year. Among this small portion of tax returns which claim charity tax credits, the median donation level remained unchanged at $250. By 2009, this rate of tax returns claiming a tax credit had dropped to 23.1%, and the median claimed level of money was unchanged at $250. These numbers are low in absolute terms, and are not keeping pace with inflation, nor the growth in our population and the growth in wealth.

Why is it that the lower-income households who can least afford to donate give a higher percentage of their income than households with $100,000+ income? Perhaps the lack of knowledge Canadians have about what they should be giving and volunteering is part of the answer. In the Ipsos study conducted for this book, *three quarters of adults said they are vague or had no idea how much people in their financial situation should be giving.* That is, Canadians lack a social norm which defines the level of charity expected in our tribe. This is an important insight.

Without guidance or defined social norms for giving, we tend to give less. With respect to philanthropy, Canadians who claim to know what is appropriate to be giving and volunteering do indeed give and volunteer more than those who have no idea (almost twice as much more!). Those who were taught to give by their parents, by their religion, or some other mentor give more. Those who are more observant of their religion, with a better appreciation of social norms and responsibilities, give more.

As Canadians move away from their religion, and/or become less observant and less practicing, we see a decline in charitable behaviour. The growing group of non-religious Canadians is less often reminded of the message to be charitable and supportive of others. This correlates with less civility, and lower happiness.

In order to feel connected, accepted, helpful, fulfilled, and good about ourselves, we need to be taught to be philanthropic. Giving and volunteering adds meaning, makes us feel fulfilled and happy. It has been our natural evolutionary nature to help others in our tribe. Furthermore, Canadians want to know what levels of charity are fair and reasonable. It is important to feel we are each pulling our weight within our communities. If someone donates $500 is this a good level or a poor social performance?

IT'S NOT YOU; IT'S ME

Consumer surveys indicate that the vast majority of Canadians are familiar with the contribution of the charitable sector, respect the important function which non-profits play in society. Canadians feel the leaders in the charitable sector are trustworthy. Eighty-plus percent of Canadians agree the charitable sector is respected and important...

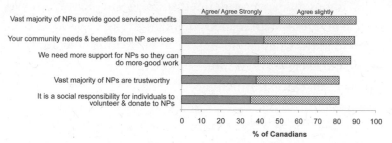

Source: Ipsos Survey of Canadian Adults, June 2010.   "NPs" = Non-Profit organizations

Our poor philanthropic behaviour is not due to a lack of respect of the sector. On average, only about 10-15% of Canadians disagree with the social and community benefits of charities.

Despite the low levels of philanthropy, there is some comfort in knowing that most Canadians do not feel they are doing enough. About three quarters of Canadians feel they are not really "pulling their weight compared to others in their socio-economic level in supporting charities in your community." At least there is some fertile soil to plant the seed that we have a responsibility to each do a little more. We will see a little later in this book, the power of each of us being just a little more charitable.

And not to put too fine a point on it, but the agnostics and atheists in Canada are the least supportive and least agreeable with the above perspectives on the non-profit sector in Canada. Those who are most religiously observant are noticeably more supportive, give more to charity, and volunteer more time. This is one reason why we need to replace the loss of religiosity in Canada with a parallel program which encourages the charitable behaviour which is slowly waning in our country. The growing group of atheists, agnostics, and non-practicing religious Canadians are not getting a message of compassion, charity, and support of others. *In the absence of religious leader-*

ship, Canadians are becoming more selfish, less generous, more cynical of charity, and less civil.

HOW MUCH TO DONATE?

Naturally, giving to charity and volunteering is a personal thing. We are each different in our wealth, free time, commitments, and so on. There is no one rule which can apply for every one. However, since we have evolved over time to observe what others do, most Canadians are interested in knowing what is the "social norm." We have an innate desire to pull our weight, and to contribute in fairness.

To answer the question, to help set an expected social norm for philanthropy in Canada, I asked Ipsos to help via a survey in May 2008, among a sample of over 1,000 regular everyday Canadian adults. In the survey, people were asked how much they felt Canadians should be giving to charity based on different income levels. Different income levels were randomly evaluated, and respondents were asked what percent of pre-tax income should be given (in their opinion) to charitable purposes. As one can likely imagine, for any one income level, there was a range of opinions. As well, answers differed as the income levels changed.

To arrive at an average level, as a useful benchmark, the middle answer was chosen for each income level. That is, the percentage of income was chosen which at least the majority of Canadians supported. This average became a higher level for higher income. In turn, I made a summary formula to allow readers to find the suggested average level for your own income:

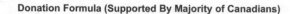

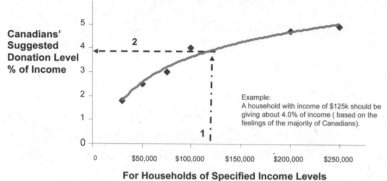

Source: Ipsos Survey of Canadian Adults, June 2010

In the more recent June 2010 Ipsos survey conducted for this book, I asked Ipsos to evaluate how Canadians felt about specifically donating 3% of income and volunteering at least 3 hours per month. Since this was close to what was discovered in the 2008 survey, I wanted to specifically assess this concept of donating 3% and volunteering 3 hours a month.

How do you feel about these levels: 3% of income, and 3 volunteered hours a month? Canadians responded favourably, overall ...

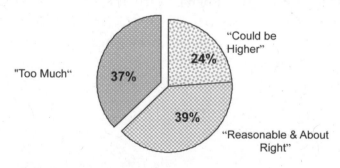

Source: Ipsos Survey of Canadian Adults, June 2010

The majority of Canadians are in support of a moral obligation to be donating 3% and volunteering 3 hours a month. Perhaps it is easier to consider this in the opposite way: *Can you live on 97% of your income?* In this light, offering just a few percentage points of income to those less well-off does not feel so painful. For those of us with much to appreciate, a few percent of income likely has an insignificant impact to our life. – Ironically, the wealthier Canadians, with more free discretionary money to spend, are less charitable in their feelings. This is also consistent with the more agnostic Canadians in society. Both sub-groups are less charitable in their behaviour as a function of their income levels...*and also less happy.*

Psychologists will say that when people help others they feel empowered because they no longer feel like victims. They're part of the solution. They are making a difference addressing the social problems they face. If we can solve problems via our own accord, through our own freedom, we can actually make ourselves happier. This gives more meaning in our lives. People who donate more in Canada do indeed feel happier. And we have already covered the latest science of brain scans showing how helping others activate our pleasure centre in the cerebral cortex. On the other hand, there is no evidence to date that I am aware of which indicates we get the same warm feeling paying our tax bills and asking the government to look after the same needy!

So we have come to the end. Thanks for reading along. I hope this has convinced you to live, think, and do some things a little differently, for your own benefit. Your happiness is in your hands. My wish for you is to live well, as nature intended (and not as the banker or corporate world wishes it). And I hope your happiness manifests itself in a happier Canada; in a nation where we help others, where we have more patience with each other, where we connect better, and where we are less stressed. Let's enjoy the simple life we so naturally crave.

To end, let me share a poem I came across which I feel is quite relevant...

"THE GUY IN THE GLASS"
By Peter "Dale" Wimbrow Sr.

When you get what you want in your struggle for pelf*
And the world makes you King for a day,
Then go to the mirror and look at yourself,
And see what that guy has to say.

For it isn't your Father, or Mother, or Wife,
Who judgment upon you must pass.
The feller whose verdict counts most in your life
Is the guy staring back from the glass.

He's the feller to please, never mind all the rest,
For he's with you clear up to the end,
And you've passed your most dangerous, difficult test
If the guy in the glass is your friend.

You may be like Jack Horner and "chisel" a plum,
And thintlass says you're only a bum
If you can't look him straight in the eye.

You can fool the whole world down the pathway of years,
And get pats on the back as you pass,
But your final reward will be heartaches and tears
If you've cheated the guy in the glass.

* **Pelf** = money or wealth, especially when regarded with contempt or acquired by reprehensible means.

Bibliography

Dawkins, Richard. *The Selfish Gene.* New York: Oxford University Press, 1976.

Dawkins, Richard. *The God Delusion.* Great Britain: Bantam Press, 2006.

De Wall, Frans. *The Age of Empathy.* New York: Harmony Books (Random House), 2009

Edwards, Michael. *Civil Society.* United Kingdom: Blackwell Publishing + Polity Press, 2004

Gilbert, Daniel. *Stumbling on Happiness.* New York, Vintage Books (Random House), 2006

Hallward, John. *Gimme! The Human Nature of Successful Marketing.* Hoboken, NJ: John Wiley & Sons, 2007

Keiningham, Timothy L., Aksoy, Lerzan. *Why Loyalty Matters.* Dallas, Texas: Benbella Books, 2009.

Keltner, Dacher. *Born to Be Good.* New York, W. W. Norton & Company, 2009.

Monroe, Kristen R. *The Heart of Altruism.* Princeton, NJ. Princeton University Press, 1996

Pallotta, Dan. *Uncharitable.* Medford, Massachusetts: Tufts University Press (University Press of New England), 2008

Wright, Robert. *The Moral Animal.* New York: First Vintage Books Edition, 1995.

Index